Let's Have Fun!

Volume 1

13 Themes to Spark Creativity

by
Rebecca Ross Klosinski

For my kids

Table of Contents

Message from the Author

Back to School

Cowboys and the Wild West

Jungle, Rainforest, Safari

Camping and the Great Outdoors

Ahoy, Pirates!

The Land of Dinosaurs

Under the Sea

Super Superheroes

Space and Aliens

Fun on the Farm

Knights, Dragons, Princesses

Eek! Monsters!

Books, Books, Books!

Patterns
Answer Key
Resources
Notes
Acknowledgements

Message from the Author

The crafts, recipes, games, etc. in this book have been imagined and refined over the last fourteen years I have spent working with kids. Some of them are tried and true classics, some of them are new spins, and all of them are tons of fun!

Whether you are a mom, a teacher, a camp leader, or a daycare provider, this collection is meant for you and your kids. My hope is that what you find within these pages will spark creativity and allow for memorable experiences. Children are naturally excited and curious and it's up to us to give them opportunities to explore.

Each chapter in *Lets' Have Fun!* features a different theme from Pirates to Dinosaurs, Farm to Ocean. Themes include crafts, games, experiments, holidays, recipes, life skills, fun facts, songs to sing, books to read, movies to watch, party ideas, costume ideas, field trip ideas, guest speaker suggestions, printable activities, and more! In the back of the back of the book you will also find resources, patterns, and samples.

So turn the page to get started and don't forget to have fun!

Rebecca

Back
to
School

Apple Stamping

Materials:

Apples

Knife

Red paint

Green paint

Paintbrushes

Paper plate

Construction paper

Instructions:

1. Cut each apple in half
2. Pour red paint onto a paper plate
3. Dip apple halves into red paint and stamp onto construction paper
4. Paint a green stem and leaf on each
5. Let dry

Note:

Apples can be stamped once, twice, or as many times as you want depending on the size of your paper. If you use multiple varieties of apples, kids can compare what the different cores look like!

Warning:

Knives are for adult use only!

Paper Plate Apple Core

Materials:

White paper plates

Red paint

Brown paint

Paintbrushes

Scissors

Glue

Instructions:

1. Cut a curved piece out of both the right and left side of the paper plate so it looks like a core
2. Paint the top and bottom edges of the plate (usually the ridged part) red
3. Paint small brown seeds in the center
4. Paint
5. Glue the leaf and stem to the top of the apple
6. Let dry

More fun:

Have kids write their favorite thing about school on their apples!

Milk Carton School Bus

Materials:

1 half-gallon milk carton

4 bottle caps

Yellow paint

Black paint

White paper

Crayons or markers

Scissors

Glue

Instructions:

1. Paint the milk carton yellow
2. While the paint is drying, cut three squares of white paper for each side of the bus to look like windows
3. In each window, draw pictures of kids riding the bus
4. When dry, glue the windows to the bus
5. Paint a thin black stripe along the side of the bus
6. Paint the word "SCHOOL" along the side in black
7. Glue the four bottle cap wheels to the bus
8. Decorate with headlights, taillights, etc.

More fun:
Glue photos of the kids onto the windows

Dancing Crayon

Materials:

Any color construction paper

Black construction paper

Crayons or markers

Scissors

Pencil

Glue

Instructions:

1. Trace and cut out Crayon Patterns A and B from desired color construction paper for the body and limbs
2. Trace and cut out Crayon Pattern C from black construction paper for the accents
3. Glue the accent pieces to the body
4. Glue the arms and legs to the body
5. Draw a face on the tip of the crayon

More fun:

Write kids' names on the center of the crayon.

Movies:

Pop in Johnny Appleseed (G) or Diary of a Wimpy Kid (PG) to get in the back to school spirit.

Dried Apple Rings

Ingredients:

Apples

Sugar

Cinnamon

Apple corer

Knife

Cooking spray

Baking sheet

Directions:

1. Thoroughly wash apples
2. Carefully core each apple
3. Slice apples into thin circles
4. Spray cookie sheet with cooking spray
5. Place a layer of apple rings on the baking sheet
6. Lightly sprinkle the rings with cinnamon and sugar
7. Flip each ring over sprinkle the other side
8. Bake at 200 degrees for 2 hours

Optional:
Soak apple rings in lemon juice and water before baking to keep them from turning brown.

Fun with Chalk

- Play hopscotch
- Play tic-tac-toe
- Play connect-the-dots

Getting to Know You

- Sit in a circle and pass around a ball. Each player to catch the ball shares something about themselves with the group.
- In this circle game that helps kids learn each other's names, the first player will say his or her name aloud. The player to their right must then say their own name and the name of the first player. Continue around the circle. The last player in line will have to remember every name in the group!
- Open up a bag of M&Ms and assign each color in the bag a question. Sit kids in a circle and pass the bag around. As each kid gets the bag, they pull out an M&M and answer the question that corresponds to the color they picked. Continue until the bag is empty.

  Sample Questions:
  Red = What is your favorite subject?
  Blue = What do you want to be when you grow up?
  Green = What is your favorite TV show?
  Yellow = What is one of your special talents?
  Orange = What do you collect?
  Brown = What is your favorite thing to do on the weekend?

I Am

As happy as _____

As sad as _____

As fast as _____

As slow as _____

As small as _____

As big as _____

As noisy as _____

As quiet as _____

As brave as _____

As shy as _____

As mild as _____

As crazy as _____

As lazy as _____

As busy as _____

As weak as _____

As strong as _____

As old as _____

As young as _____

I am _____

★

Back to School Wordsearch

```
X F E D T R M L E R I T L W V
A O E E E G U B A C K P A C K
X S Q C A N Y D D N S N W U H
K P E B C L Z P U C X H R L N
U S T H H P E N C I L J A R S
S A B G E Q C S X R F E A R C
X O B C R E D H R U A E U J E
X L O Q R N B J A F L Y B U S
I J O S E S Z D V L O Q O R S
V W K I P Y T Z H P K T Y N C
R D R J A V B U D I J J O I H
V F A X P L F V D T O G W L O
G R A D E C Y B F E Y Z N L O
R X O A A Y R I M T N W B K L
Q A P P L E I R D Y A T T L R
```

APPLE
BACKPACK
BOOK
BUS
CHALK
CRAYON
DESK
FRIENDS
GRADE

LEARN
LUNCHBOX
PAPER
PENCIL
RECESS
SCHOOL
SHARE
STUDENT
TEACHER

Books

If You Take a Mouse to School by Laura Numeroff
David Goes to School by David Shannon
How Do Dinosaurs Go To School? By Jane Yolen
Back-to-School Rules by Laurie B. Friedman
First Day Jitters by Julie Danneberg
How I Spent My Summer Vacation by Mark Teague
Amelia Bedelia's First Day of School by Herman Parish

Board

No back to school board would be complete without an apple tree! Have kids trace and cut out their hands several times to make the leaves of your tree- the bigger the tree, the more hands you'll need. They can then stamp red handprints, cut them out, and add stems to make the apples. Or write their names on red construction paper apples.

Songs

The Wheels on the Bus
Down by the Bay
Five Little Frogs
Apples and Bananas
Workin' on the Railroad
Shake Your Brain
There's a Hole in my Donut

Life Skill

Healthy Eating Habits

Have kids brainstorm lists of healthy foods and unhealthy foods (or foods that should only be eaten in moderation). Talk about serving sizes and how many servings of each food group you need in a day. Have kids draw a lunchbox and fill it in with a balanced meal using in crayon or plastic food.

Photo Op

The first days and weeks of a new school year are filled with moments fit to be commemorated. Take a photo of each child holding props like apples and pencils in front of a backdrop that announces what grade they are starting. These photos will be great keepsakes. You can even take a second picture at the end of the year to see how they have grown!

Speaker

Start a new year off right by inviting a member of your school's staff to come and talk to your group or class. It could be anyone from the principal to the secretary; cafeteria workers to custodians. Each essential employee will be able to share what they do to help keep the school running.

Cowboys
and the
Wild West

Sheriff Badge
& Mustache

Materials:

Yellow fun foam

Black or brown fun foam

Scissors

Pen

Glue

Gold glitter

Paint pens

Pin backs

Skewers or craft sticks

Badge Instructions:

1. Trace a star onto yellow fun foam and cut out
2. Squeeze a line of glue around the edge of the star and sprinkle with gold glitter
3. Write kids' names in the center of the star
4. Glue pin back in place and let dry

Mustache Instructions:

1. Trace a mustache onto black or brown fun foam and cut out
2. Glue a skewer or craft stick to the back of the mustache

Photo op:
With permission, take photos of kids in their mustaches and badges!

Log Cabin

Materials:

Newspaper

Brown construction paper

Brown paint (optional)

Scissors

Glue or tape

Instructions:

1. Decide whether to create logs out of newspaper that will later be painted or out of brown construction paper
2. Cut the paper of choice into 6x7 inch strips
3. Roll each strip into a log, securing the seam with glue or tape
4. Once enough logs have been rolled, begin building the log cabin by stacking and gluing them together
5. Create a base by cutting a piece of construction paper to fit the size of your structure and gluing it into place
6. Cut two pieces of construction paper to fit for a roof
7. If you chose to use newspaper, paint the finished structure
8. Don't forget about doors and windows! These can be painted on, drawn on, or cut out and glued on

Lantern

Materials:

Milk cartons or aluminum cans

Hammer and nails

Battery operated tea lights

Paint and paintbrushes

Scissors

Skewers

Paint

Instructions for Milk Carton:

1. Thoroughly wash and dry milk cartons
2. Cut the tops off of cartons
3. Paint the outside of the carton with desired color
4. Draw a design (such as a star or horseshoe) onto all four sides
5. Using a nail or skewer, poke holes along the design
6. Place tea light inside

Instructions for Aluminum Can:

1. Thoroughly wash and dry aluminum cans
2. Cut off the top of the can. Once removed, cut small, vertical notches along the top and fold the sharp edges in
3. Draw designs on the outside
4. Use a hammer and nail to punch holes along the design
5. Paint the can with desired color
6. Add a tea light

Paper Plate Cow

Materials:

Paper plate

Brown construction paper

Tan construction paper

Large wiggly eyes

Crayons or markers

Scissors

Glue

Instructions:

1. Cut two cow ears and a round cow nose out of tan construction paper
2. Cut two horns out of brown construction paper
3. Glue ears and horns to the top of the paper plate
4. Add wiggly eyes and nose
5. Draw on nostrils and a mouth
6. The paper plate can either be colored in or have spots added to it

More fun:

Martha is an adventurous cow in No Moon, No Milk! by Chris Babcock. Glue a craft stick to paper plate cows and use them as puppets to play along with while reading the book. You can even write a story about where you think Martha will go next!

Denim Pouch

Materials:

The back pockets of jeans

Assorted ribbons, buttons, etc.

Craft paint tubes or fabric pens

Scissors

Glue

Instructions:

1. Cut pockets from the back of denim jeans, making sure to keep the front and back of the pocket together
2. Using hot glue or craft glue, attach a ribbon or a piece of yarn or rope to each corner, creating a handle
3. Write kids' names across the pocket
4. Let kids decorate their pockets with craft scraps

Cowboy Code:

A cowboy never takes unfair advantage

A cowboy never betrays a trust

A cowboy always tells the truth

A cowboy is kind and gentle

A cowboy is always helpful when someone is in trouble

A cowboy is always a good worker

A cowboy respects his parents and the law

A cowboy is patriotic

Money Management

Bank

Thoroughly wash and dry a small milk carton. Seal the top and cut a slit where coins can be deposited. Paint the outside of the milk carton light brown or red to emulate wood or brick. When dry, add doors, windows, and the word BANK to make it look like an old fashioned, western bank.

Money Management

Use a set of play money (paper currency and coins) and give each kid a set amount. Have them make three piles, one for saving, one for spending, and one for bills. They can decide how much will go in each pile and then you can discuss their choices. This is also a great time to discuss what bills are and how much things cost to buy. Older kids can even make a budget.

Basic Banking

Introduce the concepts of deposit and withdrawal. Use basic math skills to calculate balances after money is put in or taken out.

Math Game

For this game you will need coins (real or plastic). Call out an amount (15 cents, 97 cents, 1 dollar and 2 cents, etc.) and see which player or team can create that amount from their coins first.

Biscuit Pizza

Ingredients:

1 roll refrigerator biscuits

1 cup pizza sauce

1 cup mozzarella cheese, shredded

9x13 glass baking dish

Cooking spray

Directions:

1. Preheat oven to 375 degrees
2. Cut each biscuit into quarters
3. Spray baking dish with cooking spray
4. Fill the bottom of the baking dish with biscuit pieces
5. Cover biscuits with pizza sauce
6. Sprinkle cheese over the top
7. Bake for approximately 20 minutes
8. Let cool
9. Pull biscuit pizza apart and eat!

Optional:

Add pepperoni cut into small pieces (or any other pizza topping that you like!) before you sprinkle the cheese to add another layer of flavor.

Horseshoes

This game requires nothing more than a little bit of space and a horseshoe set!

Hula Hoop Spear Game

For this turn-of-the-century favorite, one player rolls a hula hoop while a second player throws a dowel or stick and tries to make it through the center of the hoop as it passes by.

Horserace

If you happen to have a couple of stick horses handy, great! If not, they can be created by folding over the top of a pool noodle (to make the horse's head) and attaching a piece of rope for reigns. Then let the races begin!

Barrel Race

Arrange a series of cones or chairs and have kids race around them on their stick horses. The fastest time wins!

Calf Roping

If you're feeling handy, you can make a calf out of sawhorses and boards painted with cow spots. If not, fasten a stuffed cow (or cow cut-out) to the top of a short pole or spike hammered into the ground. Use a small, rope-wrapped hula hoop as the lasso and let little buckaroos try their hand.

Cowboy Day

Decorations

Place hay bales all around the room and decorate the walls with cactus and horseshoe cutouts. Cover tables with bandanas.

Dress Up

Have kids come dressed up in their best cowboy/cowgirl/rodeo gear: cowboy hats, cowboy boots, bandanas, jeans, plaid shirts, etc.

Grub*

Serve up some Cowboy Beans (baked beans) in tin cans and cornbread in pie tins. Try some ice cold root beer or a Purple Cow (vanilla ice cream and grape soda).

Activities

Let little cowpokes try panning for gold. Fill a tub with about two inches of sand, mix in gold nuggets (rocks painted gold) and cover with water. Use a pie tin to swish around and collect the nuggets.

Games

Play Hula Hoop Spear, Horse Race, Barrel Race, or Calf Roping

Music

Pop in a kid's country CD to set the mood. Or teach kids how to square dance and have a hootin', hollerin' good time!

Favors

Give out gold nugget gum in bags with dollar signs drawn on them.

*more grub in Recipes

WANTED

Tall Tale

Once upon a time there was a man named _____.
(name)

He lived in _____. One day he and his pet
(city)

_____ _____ decided it was time to go on
(animal)   (pet name)

an adventure. So they packed up their _____
(plural noun)

and drove off in their _____. They traveled to
(vehicle)

many exciting places like _____ and _____.
(place)   (place)

They also made friends like _____ the _____
(name)   (job title)

and _____ the _____. They traveled for
(name)   (job title)

_____ before they got back home. When they
(amount of time)

arrived, _____ said, "_____!"
(man's name)   (exclamation)

Tall Tale

Name _____

City _____

Animal_____

Pet Name _____

Plural Noun _____

Vehicle _____

City _____

City _____

Name_____

Jon Title _____

Name _____

Job Title _____

Amount of time _____

Name from line 1 _____

Exclamation _____

Movies

Toy Story 2 (G)

The Indian in the Cupboard (PG)

All About Cowboys for Kids (NR)

Tall Tale (PG)

Elmo's World: Wild Wild West! (TVY)

Cowgirl Dora (TVY)

Home on the Range (PG)

Terms

Cattle drive – to move a herd of cattle

Chuck wagon – food wagon

Hanker – to want something

Mosey – to leave slowly

Rodeo – a competition of cowboy skills

Wrangler – an animal handler

Yee-Haw! – an exclamation of excitement

Books

Cowboy Camp by Tammi Sauer

Cowboy Bunnies by Christine Loomis

The Brave Cowboy by Joan Walsh Anglund

The Dirty Cowboy by Adam Rex

Cowboy Small by Lois Lenski

Cowboy Slim by Julie Danneberg

Little Red Cowboy Hat by Susan Lowell

Songs

Home on the Range
Skip to My Lou
On Top of Old Smokey
Happy Trails
I'm an Old Cowhand
Get Along Little Dogies
Back in the Saddle Again

Fun Facts

Buffalo Bill started his famous Wild West Show in 1883
Annie Oakley was famous for her sharpshooting skills
Gene Autry was known as the "Singing Cowboy"
Will Rogers was a trick rider known for witty quips
John Wayne acted in 180 cowboy films
Roy Rogers & Dale Evans were a husband and wife
 duo who performed with their horse Trigger

Speakers

Have members of the local 4H Club come and visit the class - they can share what it's like to care for horses, cows, pigs, and even rabbits.

Contact your nearest rodeo grounds to arrange for riders to come and talk about (or even demonstrate!) their skills.

Jungle, Rainforest, Safari

Zoo Passport

Materials:

White computer paper

Construction paper

Scissors

Markers or crayons

Instructions:

1. Cut sheets of 8 ½ x 11 computer paper into quarters – as many sheets as desired

2. Brainstorm a list of zoo animals to write on the board as reference

3. On each quarter sheet, have kids draw different animals from the list and write the names of each underneath

4. Someone with artistic skill can demonstrate how to draw animals, kids can use books as reference, or they can simply use their imaginations!

5. Cut construction paper covers to fit the sheets and staple the pages inside. Leave a blank page in the front for kids to write their names as well as the name of a zoo they might visit.

6. Leave a few blank pages in the back for notes or more animals

7. Place a sheet of star stickers inside each. When kids find an animal, they can put a sticker next to it

Swirly Snake

Materials:

Paper plates or colored construction paper

Paint (greens, yellows, etc.)

Red construction paper

Wiggly eyes

Sequins or glitter

Glue

Scissors

Instructions:

1. If using a paper plate, have kids paint the plate first with their choice of snake color. When dry they can paint snake stripes/designs

2. If using a piece of colored construction paper, cut into a circle roughly the size of the paper plate and have kids paint or color it with their choice of snake stripes/designs

3. Cut a spiral in the circle/plate beginning at the outside edge and working around in toward the center

4. Once cut, kids can further decorate their snakes with sequins and glitter

5. Cut a forked tongue from red construction paper and glue to the head end of the spiral

6. Glue on two small wiggly eyes

More fun:

Bring in close-up pictures of snake skins in various colors and patterns

Handprint Elephant

Materials:

Gray paint

Black paint

Green paint

Paintbrushes or paper plates

White construction paper

Small wiggly eyes

Gray construction paper (optional)

Scissors (optional)

Glue (optional)

Instructions:

1. Paint kids' hands gray. Or they can dip their hands in paint that has been poured onto a paper plate
2. Have kids stamp their hand in the center of a white piece of construction paper upside down – the fingers will be the elephant's legs, the thumb will be the trunk
3. When dry, paint small black hooves at the ends of the legs and draw or paint a small tail
4. The ear can either be drawn on or cut from gray construction paper and glued in place
5. Glue on eyes
6. For an added touch, have kids paint grass underneath their elephant

Talking Crocodile

Materials:

Green construction paper

White construction paper

Crayons or markers

Glue

Scissors

Hole Punch

Paper fasteners

Instructions:

1. Trace and cut out Crocodile Patterns A and B from green construction paper
2. Punch a hole through the X in each pattern
3. Glue a row of teeth cut from white construction paper to the top and bottom jaws
4. Attach the two pieces together with a paper fastener
5. Draw on eyes and scales

Fun Facts:

Crocodiles vs. Alligators

- *Both are members of the reptilian order Crocodylia*
- *Neither bother to chew their food before swallowing*
- *The only place you will find gators <u>and</u> crocs is in Florida*
- *Crocs have long, pointed snouts and gators have rounded snouts*

Toucan

Materials:

Teal construction paper

Yellow and pink paint

Paintbrushes

Assorted feathers

Large wiggly eyes

Orange pipe cleaners

Scissors

Glue

Instructions:

1. Trace and cut out Toucan Pattern A
2. Paint the beak with yellow and pink stripes
3. Glue a single feather to the top of the head
4. Add several feathers to the tail
5. Glue one large eye in place
6. Add pipe cleaner claws to the bottom

More fun:

Toucan Sam is the mascot for Froot Loops cereal. Froot Loops make fun, edible beads for necklaces! There are eight colors to choose from so kids can create endless color combinations and patterns.

Safari Gear

Vest

Safari vests can be made by removing the bottom from a large paper bag and cutting a slit down the front and two holes for arms.

Necklace

Make a tribal necklace by cutting leaves and flowers out of construction paper and then threading them on a string with uncooked penne pasta.

Mask

Cut out tribal face masks from construction paper and make holes for the eyes, nose, and mouth. Have kids decorate with macaroni, beads, and small twigs.

Binoculars

Create binoculars by attaching two toilet paper rolls side by side, decorating them, and punching two holes for a strap made of string.

Compass

Cut circles from white fun foam and punch a hole in the center. Cut arrows from red construction paper and attach them to the center of the circle using a paper fastener. Kids can then write N, S, E, and W on their compasses and begin exploring!

Tarzan Says

A jungle-themed version of Simon Says – make sure "Simon" throws in lots of animal sounds and movements!

Centipede Tag

A twist on conventional tag, when a player is tagged they have to join hands with the player that tagged them instead of being out. Soon a long line of players will be running around tagging those that are left.

Hippo, Hippo, Lion

A variation of Duck, Duck, Goose fit for little explorers on safari.

Elephant Races

Pairs of players stand back to back on a broomstick and run toward the finish line. Teamwork wins this race!

Monkey Bar Races

Send little monkeys racing across this piece of playground equipment.

Ostrich Egg* Relay

Have players race, holding a spoon in their mouth with a (hardboiled) egg balanced on the end.

Chalk Tracks

Pass out chalk and pictures of animal tracks and let kids draw their own trails along the sidewalk.

*Not a real ostrich egg, although bringing one in to share would be tons of fun!

Banana Ice Cream

Ingredients:

Bananas

Knife

Blender

Directions:

1. Cut bananas into slices
2. Freeze slices for 1-2 hours
3. Place slices in a blender and blend

Optional:

Add a small scoop of peanut butter or a dash of cocoa powder.

Fruit Kabobs

Ingredients:

Various fruits (kiwi, apple, banana, etc.)

Skewers

Directions:

1. Cut fruits into slices or chunks
2. Lay pieces out on trays and have kids choose their favorites
3. Pass out skewers and lets them stack their own kabobs

Books

The Rainforest Grew All Around by Susan K. Mitchell
We're Roaming in the Rainforest by Laurie Krebs
If I Ran the Rainforest by Bonnie Worth
Rumble in the Jungle by Giles Andreae
Way Far Away on a Wild Safari by Jan Peck
Giraffes Can't Dance by Giles Andreae
The Very Busy Spider by Eric Carle

Movies

Tarzan (G)
The Lion King (G)
Over the Hedge (PG)
The Jungle Book (G)
FernGully: The Last Rainforest (G)
George of the Jungle (PG)
Swiss Family Robinson (NR)

Field Trip

Visit the zoo! Many cities have a zoo or one close enough to visit on a day trip. Reserve a group tour and don't forget to take your passports!

If you can't get to the zoo, have the zoo come to you! Do a quick internet search for handlers that can bring their animals to your school.

Life Skill

Exploring

Bring in real, working compasses for kids to experiment with. Explain north, south, east, and west and send them on a type of scavenger hunt using paces and compass directions. Break into groups and have each one design a map that another group will try to follow.

Board

Surround your bulletin board in large leaves and flowers to make it feel like a jungle. Have each kid color a face with a safari hat that you can then place inside an amazon cruising boat you have designed. For an added touch, put crocodiles in the water or monkeys swinging from vines.

Extras

Bring in coconuts to cut open and try
Have kids decorate the room with leaves and vines
Make giant tropical flowers out of tissue paper
Make rain sticks out of paper towel tubes stuck with
  toothpicks and filled with beans
Have kids draw themselves as explorers and tell you
  where they would go on their own expedition

Camping
and the
Great Outdoors

Leaf Rub

Materials:

Leaves

Items from nature

White paper

Crayons

Instructions:

1. Have kids collect leaves and other items from nature that have interesting textures
2. Pass out crayons that have had their wrappers removed and pieces of white paper
3. Choose a leaf and lay a piece of paper over the top of it
4. Using the side of the crayon (not the tip) rub over the paper. Impressions will slowly begin to appear
5. Repeat with other items

More fun:
Rub many different items on the page to create a collage
Collect items not found in nature and compare the rubbings
Try to guess what items will look like before you rub them

Even more fun:
Instead of throwing the leaves and twigs away, create a piece of nature art!

Pet Rock

Materials:

Medium sized rocks

Cardboard

Hot glue

White glue

Craft paint

Craft scraps

Scissors

Wiggly eyes

Instructions:

1. Collect rocks from outdoors or purchase a bag from the craft store. Rocks should be large enough to fill the palm of a child's hand
2. Hot glue each rock to a square of cardboard for a base
3. Decorate pet rocks with paint, pieces of yarn, or other craft scraps. Add mouths, ears, hair, clothes, accessories, anything!
4. Glue on wiggly eyes
5. When finished, have kids name their pets and write the name on the piece of cardboard

Bird Feeder

Materials:

Toilet paper rolls

Peanut butter

Plastic knife

Birdseed

Plate

Hole punch

String

Instructions:

1. Punch two holes in either side of the top of the toilet paper roll
2. Thread a piece of string through the holes and tie the ends together. This will be used to hang the birdfeeder when it is finished
3. Spread peanut butter all over the outside of the toilet paper roll
4. Pour birdseed onto a plate
5. Roll the peanut butter-covered toilet paper roll in the birdseed
6. Hang birdfeeder for birds to enjoy!

Warning:
Be careful of peanut allergies!

Variation:
A simple flour and water paste can be used to adhere seeds instead of peanut butter

Handprint Campfire

Materials:

Black or dark blue construction paper

Yellow paint

Orange paint

Brown paint

Paintbrushes

Paper plates

Instructions:

1. Use a piece of black or blue construction paper to emulate the night sky
2. Pour orange paint onto a paper plate and have kids dip their hands into it
3. Stamp hands several times in the center of the construction paper to make flames
4. Repeat the painting process with yellow paint, stamping the yellow right over the top of the orange
5. When dry, paint underneath the flames to make the campfire
6. For added detail, have kids paint yellow stars in the sky or use shiny star stickers

More fun:

Serve up some hot cocoa to go with your toasty campfires!

Owl

Materials:

Construction paper in three colors

Crayons or markers

Scissors

Glue

Instructions:

1. Trace and cut Owl Pattern A from one color of construction paper for the owl's body
2. Trace and cut Owl Pattern B from a second, complimentary color of construction paper for the wings and eyes. For example, if using dark blue for the owl's body, use light blue for the accents. Try fun color combinations like orange and yellow, pink and red, purple and violet
3. Trace and cut Owl Pattern C from orange construction paper for the beak
4. Glue the wings, eyes, and beak in place
5. Draw a dot in the center of each eye
6. Draw several rows of "V"s across the owl's stomach to look like feathers

Bulletin Board:

Make a big tree on your bulletin board and put these colorful owls on the branches. Add the words "Whooo loves camping?!" You can even put your Happy Campers at the bottom of the board under the tree!

Happy Camper

Materials:

Construction paper, any color

Camera

Scissors

Glue

Instructions:

1. Trace and cut out Happy Camper Pattern A from construction paper. Each kids will need two
2. In the center of the bottom of one of the triangles, cut a slit roughly halfway up
3. Fold back the sides of the slit to approximate tent flaps
4. Glue the second triangle to the back of the first, being careful not to glue the tent flaps down
5. Take pictures of the kids as if they were lying down peeking out of the tent
6. Print the photos in a size that will fit inside the tent opening and cut out little campers
7. Glue the photos inside the tent flaps

Campfire Brownies

Ingredients:

Brownie mix

Bag of oranges

Barbecue

Spoon

Foil

Oven mitts

Directions:

1. Prepare brownie mix according to the instructions on the box
2. Set up your barbecue or campfire
3. Cut the tops off of the oranges and scoop out the fruit, leaving the skin intact. Save the tops
4. Fill the oranges with brownie mix just past halfway
5. Replace the orange tops and wrap the oranges in foil
6. Place the foil-wrapped oranges in the coals of your barbecue or campfire
7. Bake for approximately 60 minutes
8. Remove oranges from coals using oven mitts
9. Set aside and let cool.
10. When cool, peel away the foil, remove the top, and enjoy!

Variation:

If you would rather use your oven, bake for 60 minutes at 350 degrees. All other instructions are the same.

S'More Pops

Ingredients:

Large marshmallows

Melting chocolate

Graham crackers

Large toothpicks or lollipop sticks

Glass bowl

Spoon

Wax paper

Baking sheet

Directions:

1. Melt chocolate in a glass bowl in the microwave according to package instructions
2. Dip one end of the toothpicks or sticks in the melted chocolate and then poke into the marshmallows
3. Crush graham crackers while sticks set
4. Dip each marshmallow into the melted chocolate and then roll in the crushed graham cracker
5. Eat warm or place on a wax paper lined baking sheet and place in the refrigerator to cool

More fun:

You can also make traditional s'mores in the microwave by stacking graham cracker squares, pieces of chocolate bar, and marshmallows on a paper plate and heating in ten second increments

Trail Mix

Ingredients:

Peanuts

Raisins

M&Ms

Materials:

Bowl

Spoon

Baggies

For traditional GORP (Good Old Raisins and Peanuts), let kids pour peanuts, raisins, and M&Ms into a bowl and stir. Divide the mix into individual baggies so kids can snack away.

For more creative trail mix, have kids bring in their favorite snack items. It could be granola, chocolate chips, or dried cranberries. Anything goes with trail mix! Try cashews instead of raisins, peanut butter candies instead of M&Ms, or dried apple bits instead of raisins.

Warning:

Be extremely careful of peanut allergies. If you know that one of your kids is allergic, eliminate all nut-related items entirely.

Scavenger Hunt w/ trail tote and magnifying glass

Take the list found on the following page, break into groups, and go on a nature scavenger hunt. To make the hunt even more fun, give kids plastic magnifying glasses and empty egg cartons that they have decorated to store their finds in.

Fort Building

Fort building is one of the greatest things about being a kid. Pile blankets and pillows in the middle of the room (along with building supplies: tape, clothespins, rope, etc.) and let them use their imaginations (and a few pieces of furniture) to create their ultimate fort.

Flashlight Ghost Stories

Camping just wouldn't be camping without ghost stories! Turn down the lights and have kids sit in a circle around a "campfire". Each little camper takes a turn holding the flashlight to tell their part of a scary ghost story. After thirty seconds they must pass the flashlight to the next person in line who will then continue the story.

Shadow Puppets

Set up a flashlight or overhead projector and let kids experiment with shadow puppet shapes or bring in a book of ideas for them to try.

Nature Scavenger Hunt

A long blade of grass
A brown leaf
A green leaf
A pine needle
A pine cone
A small stick
A small rock
A feather
A clover
A piece of bark
A piece of litter
Something round
Something smooth
Something rough
Something that makes noise
Something beautiful

Total # of items found _____

*Don't forget to wear gloves or wash your hands when you're done!

Books

More Bears! By Kenn Nesbitt

Olivia Goes Camping by Alex Harvey

The Bear Scouts by Stan and Jan Berenstain

Sounds of the Wild: Birds by Maurice Pledger

Scaredy Squirrel Goes Camping by Melanie Watt

A Camping Spree with Mr. Magee by Chris Van Dusen

The Very Lonely Firefly by Eric Carle

Life Skill

First Aid

Teach kids basic first aid skills like how to stop a wound from bleeding, how to apply a bandage, and what to do in case of a real emergency (call 911!). Older kids can learn CPR and how to do the heimlich maneuver. Younger kids can experiment with first aid supplies and learn what to do if they get burned.

Extras

Add more to your camping experience:

Put up a paw print identification chart

Find out what plants to avoid in the wilderness

Show how to use an acorn as a whistle

Let kids count the rings inside a slice of tree

Tell about your favorite outdoor experience

Watch Open Season or Yogi Bear

Centers

Setting up a dramatic play area for camping is a snap! Bring in a small, two-person tent for your centerpiece and surround it with chairs or a picnic table, camping dishes, sleeping bags, miscellaneous camping gear, and a campfire made from a circle of rocks, paper bag rolled logs, and orange tissue paper flames.

Holiday

Did you know that the fourth Saturday in June is Great American Backyard Campout Day? It is! The National Wildlife Federation encourages families to celebrate by spending time outdoors – set up a tent in the backyard and sleep under the stars. For kids who have never been camping, this will make a great introduction to the activity.

Speaker

Boy Scouts make great guest speakers because they know all about camping and survival skills. Not only can they share with your class what it's like to camp in the wilderness, they can also show them how to tie knots, how to use a compass, how to pitch a tent, how to pack for a hiking trip, and more. They may even have some great camping stories!

Ahoy,
Pirates!

Handprint Pirate

Materials:

Black paint

Skin-tone paint

Red paint

Paintbrushes

Construction paper, any color

Instructions:

1. Have kids wash their hands before beginning
2. Using a paintbrush, paint the palm of each kid's hand with a skin-toned paint and the fingers with black paint
3. Press hands down on a piece of construction paper so that the fingers are pointing downward. Be careful to keep the thumb tucked in close
4. When the handprints are dry, paint on pirate bandanas in black and red
5. Paint pirate faces onto the palms
6. For an extra touch, paint snarling teeth or stubble on the faces
7. When dry, cut pirates out

More fun:

Glue pirates to white construction paper and add a background scene with palm trees, treasure chests, etc.

Pirate Flag

Materials:

White paper

Black construction paper

Black markers or crayons

Skewers

Glue or tape

Instructions:

1. Draw a skull and crossbones
2. Display a traditional skull and crossbones flag that kids can look at for reference
3. When drawing their personal skull and crossbones, encourage them to add details as they would in a self portrait
4. Cut out the skull and glue to a rectangular black construction paper pirate flag
5. Glue or tape a skewer to the side of the flag for easy waving

Examples of personal touches:

If a child is an artist, their crossbones can be paintbrushes

If a child wears glasses, add them to the skull

If a child is known for her ponytail, add one on

If a child has a favorite hobby, incorporate it into the flag

If a child has a favorite item, it can be added as a charm dangling from the skull or the crossbones

Tattooed Banana

Materials:

Bananas

Toothpicks

Black felt

Cloth scraps

Instructions:

1. Give each kid a banana, still in the peel
2. Pass out toothpicks
3. Have kids draw designs on their bananas by applying gentle pressure with their toothpicks so as not to pierce the skin. They can draw pictures, patterns, write words, etc. Make sure that they leave a spot at the top of the banana for drawing a face
4. Explain that, at first, they will not be able to see what they are drawing
5. Set bananas aside for about fifteen minutes
6. After fifteen minutes, check the bananas. Kids will be surprised to see that their designs are now visible!
7. Once ready, they can dress up their bananas as tattooed pirates by adding black felt eye patches and tying bandanas around their "necks"
8. Bananas can be taken home to eat or eaten right away

Message in a Bottle

Materials:

Plastic water bottles

Off-white paper

Brown watercolor paint

Brown crayon or marker

Red crayon or marker

Instructions:

1. Wash and thoroughly dry water bottles
2. Pass out sheets of off-white paper cut to fit inside the bottles
3. Carefully tear a thin strip along each of the four edges of the paper to create a worn look
4. Paint a watered down line of brown watercolor around the edges of the paper
5. Let dry
6. Once dry, crumple up the paper and then smooth flat again
7. Draw a treasure map using a brown marker or crayon and add a red "X"
8. Roll up the paper and slip it inside the bottle. Replace cap
9. Decorate the outside of the bottles for an added touch

Variation:

Write a letter on the paper instead of drawing a map or write a pirate story

Mermaid

Materials:

Seafoam green construction paper
  (substitute with pink, aqua, or purple if desired)
Yellow, brown, or orange-red construction paper
Skin-tone construction paper
Pencil
Scissors
Crayons
Glue
Glitter

Instructions:

1. Trace and cut out Mermaid Pattern A (body) from skin-tone, Mermaid Pattern B (tail) from seafoam, and Mermaid Pattern C (hair) from yellow, brown, or orange-red construction paper
2. Draw on faces
3. Glue the hair to the back of the head portion of the body and glue the tail to the front side of the body
4. Using glue, draw scales on the tail of the mermaid
5. Sprinkle glitter over the glue to create shiny scales

Petey Parrot

Materials:

White construction paper

Yellow construction paper

Red paint

Orange paint

Green feathers

Wiggly eyes

Paintbrushes

Scissors

Glue

Instructions:

1. Paint the bottom of kids' feet red with orange toes
2. Stamp feet onto white construction paper
3. The red will be the body of the parrot and the orange will be the claws
4. Glue a feather to the top of the parrot's head
5. Glue feathers to the side of the parrot's body for wings
6. Glue wiggly eyes in place
7. Cut out a beak from yellow construction paper and glue in place
8. For fun, draw on a black eye patch to make Petey a pirate!

Fun Fact:

Some parrot species can live to be over 80 years old!

Pirate Day!

Decorations

Decorate your space with skull and crossbones flags, gold coins, jewels, overturned treasure chests, palm trees, parrots, and pirate ships. Add netting and sea creatures for an extra touch.

Dress Up

Have kids come dressed in their best pirate garb – vests, eye patches, bandanas, and tattered shirts and pants.

Activities

Use face paint to give the kids stubbly beards. You can also have them make their own pirate hooks out of tin foil, telescopes out of paper towel tubes, and eye patches out of black felt. Don't forget to try out the pirate lingo found at the end of this chapter and invent pirate names like Sally the Seasick or Blackbeard Brandon.

Games*

It wouldn't be Pirate Day without a treasure hunt! Divide kids into teams and provide them with maps. Each map should end with an "X" in a different location so that each team can find a treasure chest filled with booty.

Snacks

Check out the next page for great party food ideas!

Music

Listen to the Pirates of the Caribbean soundtrack to get in the spirit!

*more games can be found in Games

Pirate Grub

Pirate Grog

Apple juice served in mugs

Seaweed

Cooked green spaghetti noodles

Cannonballs

Black olives speared with sword picks

Octopus

Hot dogs with the bottom half sliced into tentacles

Ships on the Sea

Boats made from orange wedges floating in a clear cup of blue jello
Add colorful sails to toothpicks to stick in the orange wedges

Turkey Legs

Substitute chicken drumsticks for actual turkey legs

Treasure Maps

Sugar cookies baked ahead of time in the shape of a square
Let kids frost with white royal icing. When the icing has set, they can
draw their own treasure maps using small tubes of gel icing or
markers that are made with edible ink for cookie decorating

Favors

Fill bags with goldfish crackers and chocolate doubloons for kids to
take home at the end of the party

Cannonball Pop

Cover two cardboard boxes in colored paper. Draw a canon on the front of each and fill with black balloons that have been blown up – these are the cannon balls. Divide the group into two teams and line them up in front of the boxes. At the signal, the first player in line will run to their box, pop a balloon, and run back to tag the next player in line. Move down the line until all balloons are popped. The first group to pop all of their "cannonballs" wins!

Walk the Plank Relay

For this game you can use a board or, if you don't have a board, a broomstick. In relay fashion, teams will cross the "plank" one member at a time (without falling into the "ocean"!). The first team to get all players across successfully wins. Combine with Cannonball Pop for a longer relay!

Parrot

This game is played like a traditional game of Telephone in which all players sit in a line and the first player is given a sentence to say. He or she then whispers the sentence in the ear of the player next to them, who whispers it to the next player, and so on. The last one in line has to say the sentence out loud – you'll be surprised at how much it will change!

Books

Pirate Princess by Sudipta Bardhan-Quallen

Pirate Pete by Kim Kennedy

How I Became a Pirate by Melinda Long

The Pirates Next Door by Jonny Duddle

Do Pirates Take Baths? by Kathy Tucker

Pirates Don't Take Baths by John Segal

Pirates Go to School by Corinne Demas

Holiday

September 19th is Talk Like a Pirate Day! Celebrate by learning some pirate lingo:

Ahoy = hello

Avast! = hey!

Aye = yes

Savvy = understand?

Booty = treasure

Grub = food

Buccaneer = pirate

Swashbuckler = adventurer

Matey = friend

Me bucko = my friend

Terms

Sea dog = old sailor

Shipshape = well-organized

Heave Ho = to throw out

Swab the deck = clean the ship

Thar she blows = a whale has been spotted

Blow me down! = an exclamation of surprise

Yo ho ho = a cheerful call to attention

Centers

A dramatic play area dedicated to pirates can be tons of fun! Create a pirate ship out of a large cardboard box. You can either attach a sail to the ship or you can fashion a makeshift sail that extends from the wall or ceiling over the ship. Don't forget your pirate dress-up kit, a stuffed parrot, telescope, treasure map, treasure chest, and steering wheel.

Movies

Peter Pan (G)

Muppet Treasure Island (G)

Jake and the Never Land Pirates (TVY)

Treasure Planet (PG)

The Pirates! Band of Misfits (PG)

Ice Age: Continental Drift (PG)

Hook (PG)

Speaker

If you've ever attended a Pirate Faire (often combined with a traditional Renaissance Festival) you know that most cities have a Guild or two dedicated to dressing up in authentic costumes and traveling the country. Many members speak the language, know the history, and can really put on a show. Call one up and schedule a G-rated visit.

The Land
of
Dinosaurs

Dino Dig

Materials:

Sandbox

Wooden stakes

String

Small shovels

Brushes

Paper and clipboard

Pencil

Ruler

Bucket

Plastic bones or dinosaurs

Instructions:

1. Mark out a large square in the sandbox with stakes.
2. Divide the square into 12-16 sections using string and additional stakes
3. Once the grid is created, bury small plastic dinosaurs under the sand. For older kids, try burying large plastic bones that can actually be excavated rather than simply dug up
4. Assign each kid a square within the grid and pass out tools (brushes, shovels, etc.)
5. As each piece is found, have kids measure them and record their findings (cataloging) on their clipboards. Younger kids can trace what they dig up

Name-o-Saurus

Materials:

Construction paper

Markers or crayons

Instructions:

1. Give each kid a dinosaur name. For example, Katie could be Kateasaurus or Bill could be Billadactyl

2. When dinosaur names are chosen, write them on the bottom of pieces of construction paper

3. Have kids draw what they think their dinosaur would look like. Encourage them to add scenery to their pictures as well (trees, rivers, volcanos, etc.)

4. When the pictures are complete, have them add facts about their dinosaur to the back of the page

Dino Info:

How much does my dinosaur weigh?

How tall is my dinosaur?

What does my dinosaur eat?

Is my dinosaur friendly?

Who are my dinosaur's friends?

What does my dinosaur do for fun?

Does my dinosaur have a special skill?

How does my dinosaur communicate?

Can my dinosaur swim or fly?

★

Fossil

Materials:

Clay

Plastic dinosaurs

Plastic bones

Items from nature

Instructions:

1. There are several options for this project when it comes to clay. Use modeling clay, flour-salt dough, pottery clay, etc.
2. Pass out pieces of clay and have kids choose what item they would like to make a fossil out of
3. Roll clay into a ball and then flatten it into a ½ inch thick circle
4. Press toy dinosaurs or small bones into the clay. Choose items collected from nature like leaves and sticks to create more fossils
5. After imprints have been made, let the clay dry completely

More fun:

- *Punch a hole in the top of the clay circle while it is still wet. When it is dry, thread a piece of string through the hole so it can be worn as a necklace!*
- *Let kids paint their fossils using bright dinosaur-inspired colors.*

Hungry T-Rex

Materials:

Butcher paper

Yard stick or ruler

Markers

Instructions:

1. Roll out a piece of butcher paper at least 5 feet in length
2. On the piece of butcher paper, draw an open T-Rex mouth (with the edges of the paper acting as the top and bottom jaws). A T-Rex jaw averaged 4 feet long, so measure accordingly
3. Be sure to add sharp teeth to the edges
4. When finished, the T-Rex mouth should look like it can accommodate a very large snack
5. Have kids lie down inside the T-Rex mouth with their feet at the opening to see how far inside they would fit. Mark each on the paper to see who goes deepest into it
6. Take pictures of the kids and label them "T-Rex Snack"

More fun:

Have the kids measure out and draw other parts of the T-Rex. A T-Rex eye was four inches wide, a T-Rex foot was three feet long, and a T-Rex tooth could reach up to nine inches!

Chocolate Excavation

Ingredients:

Chocolate pudding

Oreo cookies

Graham crackers

Toasted, shredded coconut

Green food coloring

Clear plastic cups

Spoons

Directions:

1. In a plastic baggie, place toasted, shredded coconut with a small amount of green food coloring and work around until color is evenly distributed. This will be the grass
2. Fill another plastic baggie with Oreo cookies and crush them. This will be the bedrock
3. Crush graham crackers using the same method. This will be the sand
4. Sprinkle crushed Oreos into the bottom of the cup
5. Add a layer of chocolate pudding. This is the soil
6. Add a layer of crushed graham cracker
7. Top off with a layer of green toasted, shredded coconut
8. Use a shovel (spoon) and dig in!

More Fun:

Bury a gummie dinosaur in the cups!

Dinosaur Bones

Ingredients:

Roll of refrigerator breadsticks

Baking sheet

Wax paper

Directions:

1. Have kids wash their hands thoroughly before beginning
2. Give each kid a piece of breadstick dough from the roll and a piece of wax paper for a work surface
3. Let them shape their dough into dinosaur bones
4. When they're finished, place the bones on a cookie sheet and bake according to package instructions
5. Let cool before serving

Dipping sauce:

Create a tasty dipping sauce for your dinosaur bones by mixing one cup of pizza sauce with ¼ cup grated parmesan cheese and a dash of Italian seasoning.

More fun:

If the dino bones are made small enough, you can use toothpicks to create a dinosaur skeleton!

Claw Grab

Lay out a large piece of plastic and dump out a bag of colorful cereal, such as Trix, and spread out. Divide players into teams, give them hair clip claws (dino claws), and assign each team a color that corresponds to a color of Trix. Teams then race to see who can pick up all of their color cereal first using only their claws. Make sure to have buckets or containers handy for clawed cereal!

Dino Races

Before the race begins, have kids make Dinosaur Feet by drawing, coloring, and cutting out large pieces of cardboard. The feet must be much larger than a kid's foot to emulate a real dino stride. Then either tape dino feet to kids' shoes or attach string handles for them to hold onto as they run. Ready, set, go!

Herbivore, Carnivore, Plant

In this dinosaur-themed version of Rock, Paper, Scissors, players will use their bodies instead of their hands to play. For this game, Carnivore eats Herbivore, Herbivore eats Plant, and Plant covers Carnivore. Put kids into two lines facing each other. Each line will turn around and confer to decide if they will be Carnivores, Herbivores, or Plants. On the count of three, both lines will turn around and reveal what they have chosen. Carnivores will show their claws, Herbivores will swish their tales, and Plants will wave their leaves. Best out of 7 rounds wins or play as long as you like.

Bubbling Volcano

Materials:

Sandbox

Vinegar

Baking soda

Red food coloring

Liquid dish soap

Instructions:

1. Have kids build a large mountain in the sand
2. Create a crater in the top of the mound of sand about three inches deep
3. Pour several spoonfuls of baking soda into the hole
4. Add one spoonful of liquid dish soap
5. Add five drops of red food coloring
6. When ready, pour about a tablespoon of vinegar into the hole and watch the lava eruption!

Warning:

Don't stand too close when the volcano explodes!

Variation:

Use a tub filled with sand or make individual volcanos from clay.

Question to ask before the experiment:

What will happen if we pour vinegar over baking soda?

Books

Dinosaurs! By Gail Gibbons

Danny and the Dinosaur by Syd Hoff

How Do Dinosaurs Eat Their Food?
 by Jane Yolen and Mark Teague

My T-Rex Has a Toothache by Elwyn Tate

Dinosaur Bones by Bob Barner

Digging up Dinosaurs by Aliki

Terms

Herbivore – a dinosaur that ate only plants

Carnivore – a dinosaur that ate other dinosaurs

Omnivore – a dino that ate plants *and* other dinos

Paleontologist – one who studies dinosaurs

Fossil – the remains of a once living thing

Microceratops – one of the smallest dinosaurs

Spinosaurus – one of the largest dinosaurs

Fun Facts

- Dinosaur means "terrible lizard" in Greek
- The first dinosaur (the Megalosaurus) was named in 1824
- Some of the largest dinosaurs (like the brachiosaurus) were actually plant eaters
- The three periods of dinosaurs are known as the Triassic, Jurassic, and Cretaceous periods

Extras

For hands-on learning, find a few visual aids to show your kids. You can bring in dinosaur teeth, dinosaur fossils, dinosaur posters, or even a sample of what a dinosaur's skin would look and feel like. For further excavation, bring in small geodes and let kids crack them open to see what's inside. Then take a trip to the natural history museum!

Experiment

The Flintstones were a family that lived in the stone ages. They used pterodactyls as airplanes, giant crabs as lawnmowers, and turtle shells as shopping carts! See how many crazy inventions your kids can imagine without using any modern technology. Have them focus on items they use in their everyday lives when creating stone age versions.

Board

For a fun, dinosaur themed bulletin board, have kids dip their hands in red, green, or blue paint and stamp upside down onto a piece of construction paper – the fingers will look like dinosaur legs and the thumb will look like a dinosaur neck. Use contrasting color thumbprints to add a spine. Cut them out and add them to a dinosaur landscape.

Under the Sea

Rock Starfish

Materials:

Pink, lime, or aqua construction paper

Bag of colorful aquarium rocks

Scissors

Glue

Instructions:

1. Trace and cut Starfish Pattern A from pink, lime, or aqua construction paper or let kids draw their own freehand
2. On each starfish, place a line of glue down the center of each arm, being careful not to fill the whole arm in with glue
3. Glue on colorful aquarium rocks
4. Let dry

Fun Fact:

Starfish, or "sea stars", are not actually fish. They live underwater like fish but do not have gills, scales, or fins so seawater is used to pump nutrients through their bodies. They may not be fish, but they do have the amazing ability to regenerate an arm if they lose one!

Ollie Octopus

Materials:

Paper towel rolls

Pink or red paint

Wiggly eyes

Markers

Glitter, any color

Scissors

Glue

Instructions:

1. Paint paper towel rolls pink or red
2. Let dry
3. Once dry, cut paper towel rolls about ¾ of the way up and repeat until there are 8 long tentacles
4. Glue on wiggly eyes
5. Add a happy face
6. Use a marker to roll each tentacle, then remove the marker and let unroll naturally
7. On each tentacle, put dots of glue going all the way up, then sprinkle with glitter – these are the octopus suckers

Note:

You may also want to paint the inside of the toilet paper roll a contrasting color, as it will show once the tentacles have been cut and curled.

Egg Carton Crab

Materials:

Egg carton

Red paint

Paintbrushes

Wiggly eyes

Red pipe cleaners

Scissors

Glue

Instructions:

1. Cut egg carton into single cups
2. Paint cups red
3. Glue on wiggly eyes
4. Cut 8 small pieces of red pipe cleaner and glue four to each side of the crab as legs
5. Cut two pieces of pipe cleaner that have been twisted into tiny claws and glue them to the front of the crab

More fun:

When the crab is dry, glue it to a piece of blue construction paper. Brush glue all around the crab and sprinkle sand over the glue. Add pieces of twisted tissue paper for seaweed or small shells to make the crab feel right at home!

Submarine Portal

Materials:

Paper plate

Silver paint

Cheerios

Goldfish crackers

Green tissue paper

Large plastic freezer bags

Blue construction paper

Scissors

Glue

Instructions:

1. Cut the middle out of the paper plate and toss
2. Paint the paper plate silver
3. Paint the Cheerios silver, about 10 per plate
4. Cut out a circle of blue construction paper the same size as the paper plate
5. Glue 5 goldfish crackers to the blue construction paper
6. Cut strips of green tissue paper, twist them into seaweed, and glue them to the blue construction paper
7. Glue the silver Cheerios all around the edge of the silver paper plate - these will act as the bolts of the portal
8. Glue one layer of the plastic freezer bag to the back of the paper plate and the blue construction paper to the back of that

Clothespin Fish

Materials:

Clothespins

Blue or green construction paper

Orange construction paper

Markers or crayons

Wiggly eyes

Toothpicks

Scissors

Glue

Instructions:

1. Trace and cut Fish Patterns A and B out of blue or green construction paper
2. Cut out one very tiny goldfish from orange construction paper
3. Decorate fish with markers or crayons
4. Glue wiggly eyes onto the big fish
5. Clip the clothespin to something that will hold it open, like a marker or a small block
6. Glue the big fish to the open end of the clothespin, being careful to place piece A to the top and B to the bottom
7. Glue the little fish to a toothpick
8. Glue the toothpick with the little fish onto the backside of the bottom of the big fish's mouth and let dry. When closing the clothespin, be careful not to squish the little fish!

Stuffed Shells

Ingredients:

Bag of large pasta shells

Variety of fillings

Paper plates

Spoons

Directions:

1. Precook large pasta shells
2. Set out a variety of fillings and let kids fill their own shells

Suggested fillings:

Cooked ground beef and shredded cheddar cheese

Pepperoni slices, pizza sauce, shredded mozzarella cheese

Cooked broccoli and cheese sauce

Cooked, shredded chicken and alfredo sauce

Crab meat and mayo

Note:

Each filled shell can be placed in the microwave or toaster oven to heat through.

Variation:

You can also bring in a bowl of small shell pasta in spaghetti sauce for a quick and easy shell snack.

Sand Dollar Cookies

Ingredients:

2/3 cup shortening

3/4 cup sugar

1 teaspoon vanilla

1 egg

4 teaspoons milk

2 cups flour

1 1/2 teaspoons baking powder

1/4 teaspoon salt

Bag sliced almonds

Baking sheet

Directions:

1. Preheat oven to 375 degrees
2. Cream together shortening, sugar, and vanilla
3. Add in the egg and milk and stir to combine
4. In a separate bowl, combine flour, salt, and baking powder
5. Slowly add the flour mixture to the wet mixture and stir
6. Chill dough for one hour in the refrigerator
7. When chilled, roll dough onto a floured surface using a rolling pin or break off small chunks and roll into 1 inch balls
8. Dough can then be cut into circles of desired size (if it has been rolled out) or pressed flat (if it has been rolled into balls)
9. Place five sliced almonds in a star pattern on top of each
10. Bake for 8-10 minutes. Edges should not be brown

Gone Fishin'

For this game, you will need a large box that has been decorated with an oceanscape. Cut away one side of the box so you are left with three walls and a floor. This is where you will keep your fish that have been made from pieces of fun foam cut into fish shapes with a loop of pipe cleaner sticking up through the middle. You will also need a fishing rod made from a dowel or long stick, a piece of string, and a hook made from a piece of wire or coat hanger attached to the end. The object of the game is to see how many fish you can hook in a given amount of time.

Friend or Foe

Which animals in the ocean are friendly to humans and which ones are not? This game will help kids learn which creatures of the deep are Friend and which are Foe. You have several options when playing Friend or Foe and can adjust the game to suit your age level or group preferences. In a simple version of this game, give kids a list of sea life (found on the following page) and have them guess Friend or Foe and write it next to the name of the creature. You could also write Friend and Foe on the board, put each fish or mammal on a card with a piece of tape stuck to the back and teams will have to race to put them on the board and see how many they place correctly. Or you could try a matching game in which a match is made up of one Friend and one Foe. Let your imagination take the lead!

Friend or Foe

Friend

Anemone

Bottlenose Dolphin

Flounder

Hermit Crab

Manatee

Sand Dollar

Sea Cucumber

Sea Horse

Sea Turtle

Shrimp

Foe

Blue-Ringed Octopus

Box Jellyfish

Fire Coral

Great White Shark

Lion Fish

Sea Snake

Squid

Stingray

Stonefish

Tiger Shark

Books

Swim! Swim! by Lerch

The Rainbow Fish by Marcus Pfister

The Pout-Pout Fish by Deborah Diesen

Commotion in the Ocean by Giles Andreae

I'm the Biggest Thing in the Ocean by Kevin Sherry

Way Down Deep in the Deep Blue Sea by Jan Peck

One Fish, Two Fish, Red Fish, Blue Fish by Dr. Seuss

Songs

Under the Sea

Down by the Bay

By the Beautiful Sea

At the Codfish Ball

Never Smile at a Crocodile

Five Little Fishies

The Octopus Song

Movies

The Little Mermaid (G)

Finding Nemo (G)

Ponyo (PG)

Shark Tale (PG)

Dolphin Tale (PG)

Disneynature: Oceans (G)

The Reef (G)

Field Trip

Visit your local aquarium or sea center to learn all about fish and the ocean. Many of these facilities will let kids feed some of the fish and most have stations where they can actually touch sea life like starfish and small, friendly sharks. If you can't get to an aquarium, try a local pet store that carries fish. Go and ask a lot of questions!

Extras

Oceans provide lots of great opportunities for hands-on learning. Bring in bottles of sand from different local beaches and let kids feel the difference. You can also bring in samples of salt water and fresh water and shells for them to feel and listen to. If anyone has a small, *portable* fish at home, let them bring it in for show and tell.

Board

Under the Sea bulletin boards are loads of fun! Decorate the bottom of your board with real sand and shells and attach the kid's crabs and starfish. Twist green tissue paper to make seaweed and add circles cut from aluminum foil to simulate bubbles. Fill your ocean with jellyfish and other sea creatures. Add seagulls and a pier to finish off.

Super Superheroes

Superhero Gear

Cape

The easiest way to make a superhero cape is by using an old t-shirt. Have kids bring in one of dad's old shirts and cut off the sleeves and front of the tee, leaving the collar intact. Or you can use a piece of fabric folded in half, cutting along the dotted line indicated on the pattern in the back of the book. Let kids decorate their capes by either ironing on pre-cut superhero logos or drawing their own using fabric markers or fabric paint.

Mask

First measure the width of a child's face. Then, using either t-shirt scraps or pieces of coordinating felt, cut a rough oval shape to size. Next, mark where the nose and eyes should go. Cut a curve for the nose and two holes for the eyes. Finally, cut a piece of elastic string to fit a child-sized head and attach each end to either side of the mask.

Cuffs

Cut an empty toilet paper roll in half and let kids decorate the two halves. They can use scraps from their cape or mask to cover them or they can color with markers or crayons. Add glitter, sequins, or lightning bolts. If the cuff is too tight for little hands to fit through, simply cut a slit up the back. A ring cut from a plastic water bottle can also be used to make cuffs.

If I Were a Superhero

Materials:

Paper

Pencils

Crayons or markers

Instructions:

1. Provide the writing prompt "If I were a superhero..."
2. Have kids draw what they would look like if they were a superhero
3. Let them decide what their superhero name would be
4. On the back of the page, write more information about their alter egos

Superhero Stats:

Name

Alias

Home base

Special Powers

Symbol/Costume

Sidekick

Nemesis

How were my powers acquired?

Does anyone know my secret identity?

Am I part of a team or do I work alone?   ★

Comic Book

Materials:

White copy paper

White construction paper

Crayons or markers

Scissors

Instructions:

1. Cut several pieces of white copy paper into quarters. These will be the pages of the comic book

2. Cut a piece of white construction paper for the cover; staple

3. Create a title, characters, and storyline for the comic book

4. Draw the comic and color it in

Tip:

Try mapping out a rough draft or storyboard of the comic first

Parts of a story:

Introduction/Beginning

Rising Action

Climax

Falling Action

Resolution/End

Characters

Plot

Setting

Conflict

Compassion

Real-Life Superhero

Superheroes make it their mission to help others. Compassion is a feeling of sympathy or empathy that one has toward those who are suffering. This feeling is often accompanied by a desire to alleviate the suffering of others in some way.

For older kids, have them write about a time when they helped someone in need or about a time when they were helped by someone else.

For younger kids, have them draw a situation in which someone helps someone else. Write their explanation at the bottom of their drawing.

Get kids thinking about ways they can help others – brainstorm random acts of kindness that can be accomplished right away and with little cost or planning such as giving a compliment or writing a thank you note.

Donation Drive

For a more involved project, find a charitable organization that your class or group would like to help and host a fundraiser or donation drive. Kids can collect eyeglasses, old cell phones, books, clothing items, canned goods, blankets, etc. Let them be a part of contacting the organization and delivering the items when done.

Superhero Training Course

Leap Tall Buildings

Set up hurdles or other obstacles that can be jumped over.

Tunnel Underground

Make a tunnel by attaching several cardboard boxes together or use tables and chairs to crawl under.

Super Speed

Sprint from point A to point B as fast as you can!

Feat of Strength

Create giant weights be tying pillows to the ends of a broomstick.

Wall Smash

Set up a pile of "bricks" made from empty cereal boxes, then use tiny fists to smash them down.

Agility test

Set up hula hoops or tires in a staggered line on the ground that can be stepped into as kids cross.

Laser Maze

String yarn back and forth across a hallway (or between four posts in the ground for an outdoor maze) in a crazy pattern and let little superheroes find their way from one end to the next.

Superhero to the Rescue

Rescue the doll from the top of the ladder!

Marshmallow Shooter

Materials:

Plastic cups

Balloons

Mini marshmallows

Scissors

Instructions:

1. Cut the bottom off of the plastic cup
2. Tie a knot in the opening of the balloon (do not blow it up)
3. Cut about ½ inch off the top of the balloon
4. Stretch the balloon over the end of the cup
5. Place several marshmallows inside the cup
6. Hold the cup in one hand and pull back on the balloon with the other
7. Let go and watch the marshmallows fly!

Tip:

For a more sturdy shooter, try doubling up the plastic cups or using a thicker yogurt container.

Variation:

Pom poms can be used instead of marshmallows.

More fun!

Set up targets for kids to shoot at

See who can launch their marshmallow the furthest.

KA-POWer Bars

Ingredients:

2 1/2 cups crispy rice cereal

2 cups quick cook oats

1/2 cup chocolate chips

1/2 cup honey

4 Tablespoons brown sugar

2/3 cup peanut butter

Directions:

1. Melt together honey, brown sugar, and peanut butter over low heat or in a microwave safe dish in 30 second increments
2. Add in the krispy rice cereal, quick cook oats, and chocolate chips
3. Pour into a 9x13 baking dish and press down firmly
4. Cut into squares or rectangles and serve

BOOM! Juice

Ingredients:

2-Liter lemon lime soda

1 packet orange flavored powdered drink mix

Pitcher and spoon

Directions:

1. Pour lemon lime soda and lime drink mix packet into pitcher and stir

Superhero Day

Decorations

Create a skyscraper skyline for a backdrop and make a flag garland from old comic books. Cut out lightning bolts and symbols belonging to Superman, Batman, Spiderman, and Captain America as well as speech bubbles that you can write "POW!" and "SPLAT!" in.

Dress Up

Have kids wear their capes, masks, and cuffs or they can come in their own costumes or superhero t-shirts.

Superhero Names

Every superhero needs a name! Have kids choose their own unique name (Alyssa the Awesome, Thunder Man, Flying Girl, Captain Billy).

Games

- Play Superpower Charades – guess the power!
- Have a laser beam battle using cans of silly string!
- Set up a training course and shoot marshmallows (see Games)

Snacks

Serve up "KAPOWer Bars" and "BOOM Juice" (see Recipes)

Favors

Dress up lollipops in capes and masks for kids to take home.

Photo Op

Fly high above the city! Find out how on the next page.

Photo Op

To create a superhero photo booth, lay down a large piece of blue butcher paper or a blue sheet. Next cut out several white clouds (about 8x10) and draw several buildings on full sheets of construction paper. Have kids put on their superhero costumes and lie on the paper or sheet so they look like they're flying over the city, then snap the photo from above.

Code

A superhero must:

Fight for justice

Protect the public from villains

Possess extraordinary abilities or powers

Have a secret identity or alias

Wear a distinctive costume or symbol

Have a sidekick, a nemesis, or both

Extras

Superheroes have many different kinds of powers: They could be a marksman, a supergenius, a teleporter, a size changer, a shapeshifter, or a time manipulator. They could be part animal, part robot, or made of armor. They could fly, have super speed, heal quickly, be invisible, use special gadgets, be trained in martial arts, or control the elements.

Books

Super Hero by E.C. Graham

Superhero School by Thierry Robberecht

Dex: The Heart of a Hero by Caralyn Buehner

Traction Man Meets Turbo Dog by Mini Grey

Captain Awesome to the Rescue by Stan Kirby

Ladybug Girl by Jacky Davis and David Soman

Eliot James, Midnight Superhero by Anne Cottringer

Speaker

A comic book artist, animator, or illustrator would be oodles of fun to have in class. These types of artists can provide a different perspective on creative expression than, say, an oil painter or a watercolorist. This is also a great opportunity to have your kids get an art lesson from a real pro. They can even share their own comic books!

Movies

The Incredibles (PG)

Zoom: Academy for Superheroes (PG)

Super Buddies (G)

Sky High (PG)

Megamind (PG)

Underdog (PG)

Bolt (PG)

Space
And
Aliens

Glow-in-the-Dark Globe

Materials:

Glow in the dark paint
  (individual squeeze bottles work best)
Clear plastic bulb ornaments
String

Instructions:

1. Cover the table you will be using to paint on
2. Pass out the ornaments, one per child
3. Carefully remove the caps from the ornaments
4. Squeeze the glow in the dark paint into the ornaments
5. Try squeezing the paint onto the inside walls and letting it slide down to create a striped effect
6. Pour out any excess paint and let dry
7. When dry, replace caps
8. Add a piece of string for easy hanging

More fun:
Don't stop at glowing globes! Use the glow in the dark paint to create pictures of space scenes. When dry, turn out the lights to reveal the full effect.

Experiment:
Did you know you can create your own glow in the dark paint using glow in the dark powder and clear paint medium?

Alien Eyeball Frame

Materials:

Foam board

Craft knife

Lime green paint

Paintbrushes

Wiggly eyes

Glue

String

Instructions:

1. Cut frames from the foam board – 8 inches by 6 inches is a good measurement to use for the outside edge.
2. Cut the opening out with a craft knife, leaving a 1 ½ inch frame
3. Paint the frames a bright, alien, lime green
4. When the paint is dry, glue wiggly eyes over the whole surface of the frame. You should see more eyeballs than green!
5. Let dry
6. Glue a piece of string to the back of the frame so it can be hung

More fun:

With permission, take photographs of the kids making silly faces. Print them out and glue them to the backs of the frames. Now you will have a ready-to-hang piece of art for the kids to take home.

Jet Pack

Materials:

2 2-liter plastic bottles

Silver paint

Red and orange felt

Scissors

Cardboard

Wide elastic

Hot glue

Scissors

Instructions:

1. Paint the empty plastic liter bottles silver and set aside
2. Cut out a square of cardboard about 10x10 inches
3. Cut two horizontal slits near the top corners and two at the bottom
4. Thread your elastic strips through these slits and secure the ends. There should be loops of elastic on one side of the cardboard that are long enough for little arms to slip through like a backpack
5. Glue the two 2-liter bottles to the other side of the cardboard square using a hot glue gun
6. Cut two large flames from the red felt and two smaller flames from the orange
7. Glue one orange flame to each red flame
8. Remove the caps from the liter bottles and glue the flames to the insides of the openings

TP Rocket

Materials:

Toilet paper rolls

Red and orange tissue paper

Construction paper

Markers or paint

String

Scissors

Hole punch

Glue

Instructions:

1. Color the toilet paper rolls to look like rockets
2. Cut strips of red and orange tissue paper
3. Glue the strips of tissue paper to the bottom of the tube rocket – these will be the launching flames
4. Cut out a circle of construction paper, making a slit from one edge to the center. Roll the circle until it forms a small, round cone. This will be the top of the rocket
5. Glue the top onto the tube
6. Punch a hole either in the side of the rocket through the roll or in the top of the cone
7. Put a string through the hole and secure
8. Decorate with markers or paint
9. Hang the rockets or let the kids fly them around the room

Moon Rocks

Ingredients:

1 bag of chocolate chips

1 small jar of peanut butter

1 jar of marshmallow fluff

3 cups crispy rice cereal

Large bowl

Spoon

Wax paper

Baking sheet

Paper plates

Directions:

1. Stir together the marshmallow and peanut butter
2. Stir in chocolate chips
3. Add crispy rice cereal
4. Hand a chunk of the mixture to each kid (on a paper plate) and let them shape it into a moon rock
5. Place all of the moon rocks on a wax paper lined baking sheet and put in the refrigerator for 30 minutes
6. Eat when chilled

Note:

Don't forget to have the kids wash their hands before they start sculpting! It may also be easier to mix with your hands instead of a spoon but, again, make sure they are thoroughly washed.

Shooting Star Quesadillas

Ingredients:

Flour tortillas

Sliced cheese

Sliced lunch meat

Star cookie cutter

Paper plates

Microwave

Directions:

1. Have kids wash their hands
2. Pass out paper plates
3. Lay out plates of flour tortillas, cheese, and meat for the kids to choose from
4. Hand out star cookie cutters (all the same size) and let them cut star shapes out of their tortillas, cheese, and meat
5. Have kids layer their stars however they would like
6. Place the star quesadillas, on their paper plates, in the microwave for approximately 30 seconds
7. Let cool and enjoy!

Variation:

You can also bake these star quesadillas in the oven. Simply place them on a baking sheet and put in a 350 degree oven for 8 minutes.

Meteor Toss

Cover a piece of foam board in black felt. Paint rings onto the felt in the style of a bullseye and add a planet to each one. Prop the board up against a wall or chair. Next, paint a small foam ball gray and cover it in strips of Velcro – this will be your meteor. The object of the game will be to toss your meteor and get it as close as you can to a planet.

Comet Tag

In this game of tag, there is a way to elude the tagger. After one player is deemed "it", the game of tag begins. If the player who is tagging reaches a certain player, that player can name a planet, constellation, or other space feature to avoid being tagged. But if they can't think of one fast enough, they get tagged and are considered "out".

Flying Saucer Frisbee

Glue together two sturdy paper plates to create a flying saucer. Cover the paper plates in foil and let little astronauts decorate them. When done, they can toss their flying saucers to one another or you can set up a course of objects that they can try to get their saucers to land on.

Space Day!

Decorations

Cover windows in black paper and paint on stars and planets. Hang green balloons with alien eyes around the room, stick up glow in the dark stars, and put out star charts.

Dress Up

Kids can dress as astronauts or aliens or they can come in khaki pants and polo shirts and wear NASA nametags.

*Games**

Have a Zero Gravity Race by having kids wear extra-large boots.

Activity

One Giant Step For Man – Have little astronauts glue a layer of gray or white sand onto a piece of construction paper. Paint the bottom of an old shoe with gray paint and stamp it onto their moon surface.

*Snacks**

Serve astronaut ice cream and orange soda for a tasty space treat!

Photo Op

Draw or paint a rocket ship on a large piece poster board or foam board. Cut out the center window for the kids to look through.

Favors

Pass out glow sticks and official Junior Astronaut certificates.

*more games and snacks can be found in Games and Recipes

What's my weight in space?

EARTH	JUPITER	MARS	MERCURY	NEPTUNE	SATURN	URANUS	VENUS
40	94.5	15	15.1	45	42.5	35.5	36.2
50	118.2	18.8	18.9	56.2	53.2	44.4	45.3
60	141.8	22.6	22.6	67.5	63.8	53.3	54.4
70	165.4	26.3	26.4	78.7	74.4	62.2	63.4
80	189.1	30.1	30.2	90	85.1	71.1	72.5
90	212.7	33.9	34	101.2	95.7	80	81.6
100	236.4	37.7	37.8	112.5	106.4	88.9	90.7
110	260	41.4	41.5	123.7	117	97.7	99.7
120	283.6	45.2	45.3	135	127.6	106.6	108.8
130	307.3	49	49.1	146.2	138.3	115.5	117.9
140	330.9	52.7	52.9	157.5	148.9	124.4	126.9
150	354.6	56.5	56.7	168.7	159.6	133.3	136

*all weights in pounds

On what planet would you weigh the most?

On what planet would you weigh the least?

On what planet is your weight closest to that on Earth?

Centers

Create the ultimate space ship! Cover a large cardboard box with white butcher paper and paint a red and blue USA logo on the side. Paint the inside black, attach glow in the dark stars, and hang Styrofoam planets. The box will sit open on its side on a table top. Attach various gadgets to make a control panel and make paper bag space helmets.

Travel

Roswell, New Mexico is popularly known for what is often referred to as the 1947 "Roswell UFO Incident" involving a supposed UFO crash. Visitors to Roswell can visit themed gift shops, an annual UFO Festival, the Robert H. Goddard Planetarium, the International UFO Museum and Research Center, and even a McDonald's shaped like a flying saucer!

Books

Man on the Moon by Simon Bartram
Roaring Rockets by Tony Mitton and Ant Parker
Personal Space Camp by Julia Cook
Me and My Place in Space by Joan Sweeney
Baloney (Henry P.) by Jon Scieszka and Lane Smith
We're Off to Look for Aliens by Colin McNaughton
That Rabbit Belongs to Emily Brown by Cressida Cowell

Speaker

Having a real life astronaut visit your group would be out of this world! But if that is out of your reach, a real life rocket scientist might be your next best bet – there are many fields of expertise involved in planning and executing space travel. Or you might have a local astronomy teacher or organization visit your class and bring their high powered telescopes!

Movies

Planet 51 (PG)

Mars Needs Moms (G)

Astro Boy (PG)

Wall-E (G)

Meet the Robinsons (G)

Toy Story (G)

The Jetsons (G)

Holidays

April 12th – International Day of Human Space Flight

April/May – National Astronomy Day

July 20th – Space Exploration Day

July 20th – First Man on the Moon

August 5th – Neil Armstrong's Birthday

October 4th -10th – World Space Week

October – Fall Space Week

Fun
on the
Farm

Muddy Pig

Materials:

Pink construction paper

Pencil

Scissors

Pink yarn

Large wiggly eyes

Chocolate pudding

Newspaper

Glue

Instructions:

1. Trace and cut out Pig Pattern A from pink construction paper
2. Cover table with old newspaper
3. Set out bowls of chocolate pudding
4. Let kids use their fingers to add chocolate pudding "mud" to their pigs
5. Glue on one large wiggly eye
6. Glue on a curly pink yarn tale
7. Let dry

Fun Fact:

Pigs like to roll around in the mud to help protect their pale skin from sunburn, to keep flies and insects from biting or bothering them, and to keep cool on a hot day since pigs can't sweat.

Cotton Ball Sheep

Materials:

Black construction paper

White pencil

Scissors

Wiggly eyes

Cotton balls

Glue

Instructions:

1. Trace and cut out Sheep Pattern A from black construction paper
2. Spread glue onto the body of the sheep
3. Apply cotton balls
4. Glue on wiggly eyes

Note:

Kids can either glue cotton balls onto their sheep just as they are or they can pull them apart and experiment with different levels of fluffiness.

More fun:

Glue completed sheep onto light blue construction paper. Let the kids draw grass for the sheep to eat. Glue down individual cotton balls and draw little legs in black crayon to create lambs (baby sheep).

Planting

Materials:

Empty milk cartons

Planting soil

Seed packets

Craft sticks

Instructions:

1. Wash and dry individual milk cartons
2. Fill each carton halfway with planting soil
3. Sprinkle in seeds of your choice
4. Cover seeds with another layer of soil
5. Write what will be growing on a craft stick
6. Place the craft stick in the soil

More fun:

Decorate milk cartons using paint, construction paper scraps, or stickers.

Variation:

For quicker results, buy seed starters (where the plant has just begun to grow) and let the kids transplant them from their original plastic container to their decorated "pots". Or plant grass seeds which grow very quickly.

Note:

Don't forget to water the plants every day!

Farm Life Painting

Use things you would find on the farm to create art!

Hay brushes

Tie or tape a handful of hay pieces onto a small stick and use as a rustic paintbrush.

Corn cob roll

Roll a corn cob in paint and then roll across a piece of paper to create an unusual pattern.

Tractor wheel roll

Use a toy tractor to make tire tracks. Simply roll the tractor in brown paint and then roll across a piece of paper.

Pumpkin stamp

Cut a mini pumpkin in half horizontally and clean out the inside. When clean, dip in paint and stamp onto paper.

Egg shell mosaic

Egg shells that have been thoroughly washed and broken into pieces make great material for mosaics. Glue the pieces down in a fun pattern or design. They can even be painted with watercolors.

Hay Bales

Ingredients:

3 tablespoons butter

4 cups mini marshmallows

6 cups crispy rice cereal

Large saucepan

9x13 baking dish

Cooking spray

Spoon

Knife

Plastic forks

Directions:

1. Melt butter in a large saucepan over low heat
2. Add in marshmallows and stir until completely melted
3. Remove from heat
4. Add crispy rice cereal and stir until thoroughly coated
5. Pour mixture into 9x13 inch pan coated with cooking spray
6. Use the back of a spoon that has been sprayed with cooking spray to press the mixture firmly into the pan
7. Let cool
8. Cut into 2x3 inch squares
9. Serve each hay bale with a plastic "pitchfork"

More fun:
Try adding sprinkles or peanut butter chips for a little bonus!

Pigs in a Blanket

Ingredients:

Refrigerated crescent rolls

Cocktail sausage links

Baking sheet

Directions:

1. Unroll the crescent dough and separate into triangles
2. Roll up one link into each crescent roll
3. Place rolls on a baking sheet
4. Bake at 375 degrees for approximately 13 minutes

Variations:

- You can also use hot dogs, sliced in half lengthwise and then cut in half or in thirds
- Add a small slice of American cheese when rolling up the crescents for a cheesy pig in a blanket

Dips:

- Make a chili cheese dip by melting together pasteurized cheese cubes and a can of chili (no beans).
- Make a mustard dip by combining 1/4 cup of yellow mustard with 2 tablespoons of honey (at room temp for easy stirring).

Churning Butter

Ingredients:

Carton of heavy cream

Salt

Baby Food Jars

Colander

Cheesecloth

Spoon

Bowl

Directions:

1. Pour heavy cream into baby food jars until they are halfway full
2. Make sure the lid is tightly secured
3. Shake the jar for about ten minutes. When it has been "churned" enough, the cream will feel like a big lump
4. Open the jar and carefully pour out the excess liquid
5. Line a colander with a piece of cheesecloth
6. Dump the butter into the lined colander
7. Rinse the butter thoroughly
8. Press the butter against the side of the colander with a spoon
9. Place the butter in a bowl, add salt to taste, and stir
10. Spoon butter back into the jar, seal, and refrigerate

Questions to ask before the experiment:

What do you think butter is made of?

What do you think will happen if we shake the cream?

Loose in the Barnyard!

For this game, blow up three packages of balloons – white, yellow, and pink. Decorate the white balloons to look like cows, the yellow balloons to look like chicks, and the pink balloons to look like pigs. Set up three crates (or use trash bags) to act as the "barns". Divide the group into three teams and have them race to see which team can get their animals back into the barn the fastest.

Milk the Cow

Fill a bucket with a gallon of milk and set on a table. A fair distance away, set up two empty milk bottles. If you can't find milk bottles, use clear plastic bottles with wide openings. Divide the group into two lines and hand the first player in each line a big sponge. On the signal, the first player will dunk their sponge in the bucket of milk, run to their empty milk bottle, and squeeze the milk into it. Continue down the line until the bottle is filled. The first to fill their bottle wins.

Potato Sack Races

Little farmers step into a potato sack or a pillowcase and hop their way toward the finish line. First one to cross wins!

Three-Legged Race

Divide the group into partners. Each set of partners stand side by side with their legs (the right leg of one and the left leg of the other) tied together just above the knee. Use teamwork to race toward the finish line.

Old MacDonald

Old MacDonald had a farm, e-i-e-i-o
And on this farm he had a cow, e-i-e-i-o
With a moo moo here, and a moo moo there
Here a moo, there a moo, everywhere a moo moo
Old MacDonald had a farm, e-i-e-i-o

Old MacDonald had a farm, e-i-e-i-o
And on this farm he had a pig, e-i-e-i-o
With an oink oink here, and an oink oink there
Here an oink, there an oink, everywhere an oink oink
Old MacDonald had a farm, e-i-e-i-o

Old MacDonald had a farm, e-i-e-i-o
And on this farm he had a sheep, e-i-e-i-o
With a baa baa here, and a baa baa there
Here a baa, there a baa, everywhere a baa baa
Old MacDonald had a farm, e-i-e-i-o

Old MacDonald had a farm, e-i-e-i-o
And on this farm he had a cow, e-i-e-i-o
With a moo moo here, and a moo moo there
Here a moo, there a moo, everywhere a moo moo
Old MacDonald had a farm, e-i-e-i-o

Old MacDonald had a farm, e-i-e-i-o
And on this farm he had a chicken, e-i-e-i-o
With a cluck cluck here, and a cluck cluck there
Here a cluck, there a cluck, everywhere a cluck cluck
Old MacDonald had a farm, e-i-e-i-o

Songs

Old MacDonald Had a Farm

The Farmer's in the Dell

Baa Baa Black Sheep

Little Bunny Foo Foo

Mary Had a Little Lamb

Six Little Ducks

B-I-N-G-O

Books

Funny Farm by Mark Teague

Sheep in a Jeep by Nancy Shaw

If You Give a Pig a Pancake by Laura Numeroff

No Moon, No Milk! by Chris Babcock

Click, Clack, Moo: Cows That Type by Doreen Cronin

The Pig Who Ran a Red Light by Paul Brett Johnson

Old MacDonald Had a Farm by Salina Yoon

Movies

Babe (G)

Barnyard (PG)

Chicken Run (G)

Animal Farm (TVPG)

Charlotte's Web (G)

Spirit: Stallion of the Cimarron (G)

The Adventures of Milo and Otis (G)

Field Trip

Get hands-on experience by visiting a real, working farm. Bale hay, milk cows, and feed pigs while learning all about farm life. If you don't have a working farm nearby, visit a farmer's market to browse and purchase fresh fruits, vegetables, eggs, and baked goods. Let your kids ask questions of the vendors to learn more.

Life Skill

Responsibility
Life on a farm requires hard work, dedication, and a strong sense of responsibility because each job on a farm is equally important. Being responsible means doing *what* you say you will, *when* you say you will. When you fulfill your obligations and are a reliable person, you are being responsible.

Extras

To give your kids a taste of farm life, set up a farm stand with fresh fruits and vegetables. Lay out corn still in the stalks, peas in their shells, and other veggies in their raw forms. Do the same with various fresh fruits. Let the kids touch and feel them, wash them, and learn how to prepare them. Then let the tasting begin!

Knights,
Dragons,
Princesses

Coat of Arms

Materials:

White paper

Pencils

Markers or crayons

Scissors

Instructions:

1. Draw a large shield onto a piece of white paper
2. Draw two lines, one horizontal and one vertical, across the shield, creating four equal sections
3. Set the shield aside
4. Have kids brainstorm what they will draw in each section to represent their lives and who they are. Sections could include hobbies, school subjects, pets, family characteristics, mottos, etc.
5. Draw one life aspect into each section and color
6. Cut out the shield

Fun Fact:

A coat of arms was used in medieval times to identify a person or family and featured unique insignia or designs. Stripes symbolized defense, acorns stood for strength, and a star represented a noble person or family. Other symbols included zig-zag lines (fire), dogs (courage or loyalty), arrows (readiness for battle), black circles (cannonballs), wavy lines (the sea), and crosses (faith).

Castle

Materials:

Toilet paper rolls

Construction paper scraps

Cardboard

Markers or crayons

Toothpicks

Scissors

Glue

Instructions:

1. Cut a square of cardboard the size you would like your castle to be (6x6 inches is a good size). This will be the base
2. Color four empty toilet paper rolls with a stone pattern
3. Glue a toilet paper roll to each corner of the base. These will be the towers
4. Create walls from construction paper scraps
5. Draw a stone pattern onto the walls, making sure to add windows and a draw-bridge
6. Glue the walls to the toilet paper rolls
7. Add construction paper cones to the top of each tower
8. Glue a small flag to four toothpicks
9. Insert the toothpicks into the tops of the four towers

More fun:

Cut out the drawbridge so it can fold open and closed!

Princess and the Pea

Materials:

White paper

Markers or crayons

Construction paper

Fabric scraps

Glue

Scissors

Split peas, dried

Instructions:

1. Draw a princess, about 2 inches tall
2. Cut the princess out and set aside
3. Cut strips of fabric from scraps for mattresses, about 1 inch by 5 inches. The more colors and patterns you have, the better your mattresses will look
4. Glue the strips of fabric onto a piece of construction paper, layering them so it looks like a stack of mattresses
5. Just below the bottom mattress, glue a spit pea
6. Just above the top mattress, glue the princess

Fun Fact:

The Princess and the Pea was first published in 1835 by Hans Christian Andersen. It has since been adapted into a stage play and a film musical. Originally a folk tale, the story of the pea-sensitive Princess has also been retold in countless versions. ★

Chainmail

Materials:

Soda can pull tabs

Wire cutters

Instructions:

1. Prepare the pull tabs by snipping through the top (the part that you pull, not the part that was attached to the can) of each one. Doing this allows each tab to be linked to another
2. Weave the tabs together by pushing one tab through the slit in another
3. Tabs can be woven in any pattern so use your imagination

Fun Fact:

Chainmail, also called "maille", was used by knights as part of their armor.

Note:

You may want to start collecting pull tabs well in advance of doing this project so you have plenty to work with.

Charity:

Ronald McDonald House collects pull tabs for charity. The tabs are collected, taken to a recycling center, and the money is then given to a local Ronald McDonald House chapter. If there are any pull tabs leftover, donate them!

Cake Pop Magic Wands

Ingredients:

Box cake mix, any flavor

Can of frosting, any flavor

Bag of melting chocolates, any flavor

Lollipop sticks

Large bowl

Sprinkles

Ribbon

Directions:

1. Bake the cake ahead of time and make sure that it is cold, or at least room temperature, before moving on to step two
2. Crumble the cake into a large bowl
3. Add about a quarter of the can of frosting and use your hands to mix (make sure they are very clean or wear gloves!)
4. Form the cake mixture into small balls. You can add a bit more frosting if they are not holding together
5. Place cake balls in the freezer for a several minutes
6. Melt the melting chocolate according to package instructions
7. Remove the cake balls from the freezer
8. Dip the tips of the lollipop sticks into the melting chocolate, then insert them into the cake balls
9. Dip the cake balls into the melting chocolate, gently swirling to let any excess chocolate drip off. Dust with sparkly sprinkles
10. Place in the freezer for several minutes to let set
11. When set, add a few strands of ribbon to finish off the wand

Dragon Fruit Pizza

Ingredients:

Sugar cookie dough

  (see recipe in Under the Sea)

Dragon fruit

8 oz. cream cheese, room temperature

2 tablespoons frozen limeade concentrate

1/2 cup powdered sugar

Directions:

1. Bake sugar cookies ahead of time or bring in dough and bake with the kids
2. Thaw the frozen limeade concentrate
3. Mix cream cheese, limeade, and powdered sugar
4. Spread the cream cheese "sauce" onto the sugar cookie "pizza crust"
5. Cut the dragon fruit into slices, being careful to cut away all outside skin first
6. Arrange the dragon fruit on the pizza

Note:

You may need more than one batch of "sauce" depending on how many kids you are serving. This serves about a dozen.

Substitution:

You can substitute kiwi (more exotic) or pear (more medieval) if dragon fruit proves too hard to find.

Catch the Dragon's Tail

Pass out strips of green cloth (or whatever color you would like your dragon to be) and have the kids tuck them into their back pockets or the waists of their pants. Instead of chasing each other in a traditional game of tag, players will try to grab each other's "tails".

Storm the Castle

Place a doll representing a Princess in a makeshift "castle". On top of the castle, place a dragon to guard her. Set up obstacles that players will have to get past in order to save the Princess from the dragon. Try a balloon moat, hurdles, a drawbridge balance beam, or quiz questions that allow players to move forward one step for each correct answer.

Cinderella's Lost Slipper

In a twist on hide-and-seek, hide a high heel shoe somewhere in your room or outdoor space. Once hidden, let little knights and princesses begin the hunt. After each minute that the shoe goes unfound, give one clue as to its whereabouts.

The Queen's Diamonds

For this game, you will need two small, empty buckets and two buckets filled with ice. Divide the group into two teams. On the count of three, one player from each team will use tongs to move the ice cube "diamonds" one at a time from the full bucket to the empty. When all of the diamonds are moved, the player will tag the next person in line on their team. Continue until one team wins.

Knight's Tunic

Using an old pillowcase, cut a circle in the bottom seam just big enough for a child's head to fit through and two holes for arms. Decorate with a fleur de lis or a cross shape.

Knight's Shield

Cut a shield from a piece of cardboard and decorate. Attach a wide ribbon or piece of cloth to the back of the shield that little knights can slip their arms through.

Knight's Sword

Cut the shape of a sword from cardboard. Decorate the handle and cover the blade with aluminum foil.

Princess Crown

Measure each princess's head and cut pieces of construction paper to fit. It's okay if it looks scrappy, because it will be covered in foil. Play with the shape to make it fit for royalty. Decorate with jewels.

Princess Scepter

Cut stars from glittery fun foam and attach to dowels or clear straws. Curl several strips of ribbon and attach at the base of the star.

Princess Tutu

Cut pieces of 1-2 inch elastic to fit each princess and sew or hot glue the ends together, creating a circle. Cut 2x24 inch strips of colored tulle. Tie the strips all the way around the elastic.

Medieval Faire

Decorations

Make flags and banners to hang around the room.

Dress Up

Come dressed as knights and princesses, of course!

Knights and Ladies

At the start of the party, knight the boys in a ceremony and bestow the title of Lady upon the girls.

Activity

Give each knight and princess a clear plastic goblet and let them decorate their cups with jewel stickers.

Tournament*

Duel – Using cardboard swords, little knights test their fencing skills
Joust – Riding stick horses, knights use their lances to hit targets
Archery – Use a plastic bow and arrow or darts to aim at targets
Tug o' War – Which team will pull the other across the line first?

Feast

Serve up grape juice in goblets and set out a buffet with medieval staples like drumsticks, sausages, rustic bread, potatoes, and carrots. Have Cake Pop Wands* and Dragon Fruit Pizza* for dessert!

Music

Play classical music to set the royal mood.

*See Recipes

Dragon Drawing Lesson

Terms

Good morrow = good day

Fare-thee-well = goodbye

Verily = very

Mayhap = maybe

Wherefore = why?

Yon = over there

Grammercy = thank you

Jobs

Many people were needed to keep a castle running. Would you have liked to be a cook? A weaver? A page? Other important jobs included artist, armorer, apothecary, astrologer, bailiff, baker, barber, blacksmith, candle maker, carpenter, chamberlain, jester, messenger, minstrel, potter, scribe, squire, chancellor, clothier, constable, gardener, and herald.

Life Skill

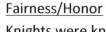

Fairness/Honor

Knights were known for being the most honorable in the kingdom. Part of being honorable is being fair and being fair means being free from bias, dishonesty, or injustice. Children often have strong opinions about fairness, so let them discuss what this means to them or act out scenarios.

Books

Dragons Love Tacos by Adam Rubin

When a Dragon Moves In by Jodi Moore

The Knight and the Dragon by Tomie dePaola

The Bravest Knight by Mercer Mayer

The Paper Bag Princess by Robert Munsch

The Princess and the Dragon by Audrey Wood

The Princess and the Pea by Lauren Child

Movies

Tangled (PG)

Sleeping Beauty (G)

Quest for Camelot (G)

The Sword in the Stone (G)

The Reluctant Dragon (G)

How to Train Your Dragon (PG)

Sofia the First: Once Upon a Princess (TVY)

Speaker

Renaissance Guilds exist all over the country and have members that are experts in medieval times. They wear elaborate costumes, speak Elizabethan English, and know the customs backwards and forwards. Any one of these members would make an excellent speaker to show your kids what it was like to live in another time.

Eek!
Monsters!

Monster in my Closet

Materials:

Construction paper

Markers or crayons

Scissors

Glue

Instructions:

1. Cut two pieces of construction paper the same size (8 ½ x 11 works well)
2. On one piece of construction paper, draw a door in the center that is about an inch smaller than the paper
3. Cut along the top, bottom, and right side of the door, but leave the left side of the door intact
4. Fold the door open
5. On the second piece of construction paper, draw a monster
6. Glue the first piece to the second, being careful not to glue the door shut
7. When dry, open and close the door to reveal the monster in the closet!

More fun:

Have kids decorate the closet doors to look like their real closets at home or to look like what they wish their closet doors looked like. Have them add details inside the closet as well, like clothes hanging, shoes on the floor, or toys in the corner.

Recycle Monsters

Materials:

Milk jugs

Plastic soda bottles

Tissue boxes

Scissors

Glue

Paper scraps

Markers

Paint

Wiggly eyes

Instructions:

1. Collect and thoroughly wash and dry empty milk jugs, empty plastic soda bottles, and empty tissues boxes and have kids choose which one they will use to create their monster

2. Tissue boxes already have an opening that works as a big monster mouth, but large holes will have to be cut into the milk jugs and soda bottles

3. Using scraps of paper and other miscellaneous craft materials (yarn, pom poms, etc.), as well as paint and/or markers, decorate the recycled items to look like monsters. Don't forget to add scary teeth, big wiggly eyes, spots, and other imaginative monster features

4. Monsters can be simple monsters or they can be taken home and used as treasure boxes

Thumbprint Monsters

Materials:

Ink pads

Paper

Markers or colored pencils

Instructions:

1. Have kids stamp their thumbs several times on a piece of paper. These will be the little monster bodies
2. Use markers or colored pencils to add eyes, horns, tails, etc. to make the monsters silly or scary

More fun:

Let the kids experiment with their thumbprints – find out what happens when you use fingers instead of thumbs!

Thumbprint Artist:

Author and artist Ed Emberley has written dozens of books for children. Many of these are drawing books for kids, including those that show how to create art using only thumbprints and fingerprints. Find out how Mr. Emberley draws monsters by visiting www.edemberleydrawingpages.blogspot.com.

Quote:

"Every child is an artist. The problem is how to remain an artist once we grow up." ~Pablo Picasso

Fuzzy Monster

Materials:

Pom Poms in a variety of sizes and colors

Felt in a variety of colors

Wiggly eyes

Pipe cleaners

Scissors

Glue

Instructions:

1. Choose a pom pom size and color
2. Choose felt and cut out two small feet
3. Glue the feet onto the bottom of the pom pom monster
4. Glue on wiggly eyes (one eye, two eyes, even three eyes!)
5. Use pipe cleaners for arms, tails, horns, or whatever the monster needs
6. Tiny pom poms can even be used for ears or a nose!

More fun:

- *Have kids write a story or facts about their little fuzzy monster on construction paper or a piece of cardboard and glue the monster to the page.*
- *Use an empty matchbox as a bed or house for the little monster to cozy up in. Give it a little blanket to make sure it's warm!*

Monster Puppet

Materials:

Paper bags

Markers or crayons

Paper scraps

Scissors

Glue

Instructions:

1. Lay the paper bag, unopened, on the table
2. Draw the parts of a monster on the bag or cut them out of construction paper and glue them on
3. Use the bottom of the paper bag to begin creating a monster – this is where the eyes, nose, and upper lip will go
4. Lift up the flap that the bottom of the bag creates when it is lying flat and put the bottom lip and tongue underneath
5. When dry, slip a hand inside the paper bag – the bottom flap is now a mouth!
6. Decorate the rest of the bag to give the monster a body

More fun:

- *Have kids write a play that their monster puppets can all act out together.*
- *Create an easy puppet show from a cardboard box or a tri-fold project board with a window cut out.*

Eye Scream Sundaes

Ingredients:

Ice cream

Toppings

Sauces

Whipped cream

Bowls

Spoons

Napkins

Directions:

1. Scoop out bowls of ice cream, any flavor
2. Set out an ice cream bar that includes sprinkles, cherries, chopped nuts, hot fudge, whipped cream, crushed cookies, gummy worms, etc.
3. Let the kids go down the line and choose the toppings for their sundaes – you can serve them or they can serve themselves

Warning:
Do not add any kind of nuts to the sundae bar if you have a child that is allergic!

Fun Fact:
July 25th is National Hot Fudge Sundae Day!

Hairy Monster Macaroons

Ingredients:

5 1/4 cups coconut flakes

1-14 oz. can sweetened condensed milk

2/3 cup flour

2 teaspoons vanilla

Baking sheet

Parchment paper

Candy for decorating

Bowl

Spoon

Directions:

1. Preheat oven to 350 degrees
2. Line a baking sheet with parchment paper
3. Mix together the coconut and flour
4. Add in the milk and vanilla
5. Form the mixture into balls (wet hands make this easy)
6. Place macaroons onto baking sheet
7. Bake 12-15 minutes, until the tops are golden brown
8. Remove from oven and take macaroons off sheet right away
10. Let cool
11. Add candy eyeballs, arms, etc. to make this hairy monster macaroon good enough to eat!

Tip: A dab of frosting is great for attaching candy features.
More fun: Dye the coconut with food coloring before using.

Pin the Eye

Draw or paint a large monster (with no eyes!) and put it up on a wall or board at a height that kids can easily reach. Next, create a large eyeball that they will attempt to stick to the right spot on the monster. Just like pin the tail on the donkey, blindfold little monsters, spin them around, and let them feel their way!

Monster Mouth

Using a piece of poster board or a cardboard box, cut out a large mouth and paint or draw on a monster. It should look like the monster has a big open mouth. Have kids stand behind a line and try to toss bean bags into the mouth.

Screams vs. Laughs

Monsters can be scary or silly. See which type of monster will win as screams compete against laughs. Divide the group into two teams, then dump out two large piles of small objects like marbles or beans and give each team an empty liter with a fill line marked on the side. On the count of three, players scramble to collect their "scream beans" or "laugh marbles" and fill their bottles. The first team to reach the fill line wins.

Eye Spy

"I spy with my monster eye..." is the name of this game. Spy items around the room and have players try to guess what they are.

Slippery Slime

Materials:

1 ½ cups clear glue

1 ½ cups liquid starch

Food coloring

Bowl

Instructions:

1. Pour clear glue into a bowl
2. Add liquid starch
3. Add food coloring
4. Mix the glue, starch, and food coloring by hand
5. Play!

Questions to ask before you begin:

What do you think will happen if we mix glue and starch?

Questions to ask after the experiment:

What do you think would happen if we used white glue instead?

What do you think would happen if we used a spoon to mix?

What do you think would happen if we made two batches using two different colors of food coloring and then mixed them together?

Warning:

Do not use a bowl that you use for food. When the experiment is finished, make sure the bowl is designated for non-food activities

Books

Where the Wild Things Are by Maurice Sendak

Leonardo, the Terrible Monster by Mo Willems

Tickle Monster by Josie Bissett

Goodnight, Little Monster by Helen Ketteman

Creepy Monsters, Sleepy Monsters by Jane Yolen

Monsters Don't Eat Broccoli by Barbara Jean Hicks

I Need My Monster by Amanda Noll

Movies

Monsters, Inc. (G)

Monsters University (G)

Monster House (PG)

Monsters vs. Aliens (PG)

Mad Monster Party (NR)

Where the Wild Things Are (PG)

The Adventures of Elmo in Grouchland (G)

Life Skill

Bravery

It's okay to be scared, but having the courage to face your fears shows bravery. Have kids paint pet rocks to look like little monsters to help them when they are scared. Let them talk about the things that scare them and how they deal with those things. Talk about the things that make them feel brave.

Board

Take a cue from the Disney film Monsters, Inc. and acknowledge the best monster "employees" in class. Print out a big sign that says "Scarer of the Month". Have kids create their own monsters out of colorful paper scraps and pin them up under the sign. Finish it off by printing out the kids' names and putting them underneath their monster personas.

Extras

Freeze Dance
Put on a CD of fun, up-tempo songs ("Monster Mash" is always a big hit!) and let the kids dance. Pause the music every 30-60 seconds or so, just as you would with musical chairs – when the music stops everyone freezes. If someone moves they are "out" and have to sit until the next song.

Photo Op

For fun photos, have kids draw big, scary monster mouths and fasten them to craft sticks to hold over their own, non-scary human mouths. Or try having kids lie down on the ground and spread their hair out and up – take the photo from above so it looks like they've just been *so* scared that their hair stood on end! Use wigs for kids with short hair.

Books, Books, Books!

Books by David Shannon

No, David!

Draw a picture of David in his blue and white striped shirt and his trademark wide grin. Underneath David, have kids write what they would like their classroom or home rules to be.

A Bad Case of Stripes

Draw a large swirly design on a piece of paper, making sure the lines crisscross several times to create spaces to color. Use crayons to color in the spaces or fill them with patterns and designs.

★*Duck on a Bike*

Have kids brainstorm a list of animals and a list of vehicles. At the bottom of a piece of paper, write "_____ on a _____". In the first space, fill in an animal and in the second space fill in a form of transportation. Then draw the unique combo.

★*How I Became a Pirate* (co-author Melinda Long)

At the bottom of a piece of paper, write "How I became a _____". In the blank space, write what each kid wants to be when they grow up. Then have them draw what they will look like.

The Rain Came Down

Create an umbrella from half of a paper plate. Use the other half to make the handle. Color the umbrella and fasten raindrops made from aluminum foil to the edges with a piece of clear fishing line.

Also read:

Oh, David!, Duck and a Book, Alice the Fairy, Too Many Toys

Books by Laura Numeroff

If You Give a Mouse a Cookie

Bake up a batch of chocolate chip cookies. Kids can be involved in the baking process or just enjoy cookies and a nice glass of milk.

If You Give a Pig a Party

Have kids draw a small, pink pig. Cut the pig out and glue to the bottom of a piece of paper. Next, have kids dip their thumbs in different colors of paint and stamp them all over the paper to create balloons. Draw several strings from the pig to the balloons. To create a more uniform look, draw a light oval over the pig that can be erased after the kids are done stamping inside it.

If You Give a Moose a Muffin

Trace each kid's foot on light brown construction paper and cut out. Trace two hands onto dark brown construction paper and cut out. Glue the hands to the top of the foot, creating antlers. At the heel end of the foot, draw a big nose and little mouth. Add wiggly eyes.

If You Give a Cat a Cupcake

Cut out a colorful cupcake using the patterns at the end of the book – one "cake" (A) and one "frosting" (B). Attach the frosting to the cake with a paper fastener so it can be swung to the side. Underneath the frosting, write each kid's unique cupcake recipe.

★*If You Give a Dog a Donut*

At the bottom of a piece of paper, write "If you give a _____ a _____". Fill in the first space with an animal, the second with food, and draw.

Books by Mo Willems

★*Don't Let the Pigeon Drive the Bus!*

At the bottom of a piece of paper, write "Don't let the _____ drive the _____". Fill an animal in the first space, a vehicle in the second, and then draw the crazy combo.

The Pigeon Finds a Hot Dog!

July 23rd is National Hot Dog Day! Celebrate with hot dogs.

Don't Let the Pigeon Stay Up Late!

Dip kids' hands in light blue-gray paint and stamp, keeping the fingers together and the thumb slightly away. Add a large eye and beak to the thumb, the fingers will be the feathers. Add feet and a nightcap.

Knuffle Bunny: A Cautionary Tale

Make a stuffed bunny from a white sock. Cut the toe of the sock down the middle to create ears and tie the base of each. Add button eyes, draw a mouth, stuff with cotton, and sew closed.

★*Today I Will Fly! (An Elephant and Piggie Book)*

Ask kids what they would be or do if anything were possible. Have them draw their wildest imaginings.

Also read:

The Pigeon Wants a Puppy!, The Duckling Gets a Cookie!?, Knuffle Bunny Too, Knuffle Bunny Free, We Are in a Book!, Naked Mole Rat Gets Dressed

Eric Carle Books

The Very Hungry Caterpillar

Create a caterpillar body by stamping a row of green handprints. At one end, stamp a red handprint for the head. Add eyes, antennae, and lots of tiny blue feet!

The Mixed-Up Chameleon

Draw a large chameleon with curling tail. Divide the tail into sections and glue different colored tissue paper squares onto each section.

Mister Seahorse

Have kids paint a piece of paper in a mix of colors. They can add glitter or bits of paper or tissue to create texture. When dry, trace a seahorse on the paper and cut out. Add a small eye.

The Tiny Seed

Use thumbprints to make a green stem and leaves and six red petals. Leave the center of the flower empty and fill it in by gluing on sunflower seeds.

Little Cloud

Mix together equal parts glue and shaving cream. Use spoons to add blobs of "cloud" onto light blue paper. For more fun, go outside, lie down, and find cloud shapes in the sky!

Also read:

The Grouchy Ladybug, A House for Hermit Crab, Animals Animals, Draw Me a Star, The Artist Who Painted a Blue Horse

Books by Dr. Seuss

★*The Cat in the Hat*

At the bottom of a piece of paper, write "The _____ in the _____". In the first space, fill in an animal and in the second space fill in an item of clothing. Have kids draw their unique combinations.

Green Eggs and Ham

Bring in slices of ham and scrambled eggs that have been made with a few drops of green food coloring.

There's a Wocket in My Pocket!

Have kids draw a Wocket and cut it out. Glue a craft stick to the back of the Wocket. Next, create a construction paper pocket that the Wocket can slide in and out of.

Gerald McBoing Boing

Have kids brainstorm as many sounds as they can think of. Then have them draw what they think these sounds look like.

Fox in Socks

Kids can create their tongue twisters using their names or share their favorite tongue twisters with the group.

Also read:

Oh, The Thinks You Can Think, The Lorax, The Sneetches and Other Stories, Horton Hears a Who!, The Butter Battle Book, The 500 Hats of Bartholomew Cubbins

Books by Audrey Wood

★*The Flying Dragon Room*

At the bottom of a piece of paper write "The _____ Room". Have the kids think of what kind of room they would like to have, fill it in the blank, and have them draw what it would look like.

★*Sweet Dream Pie* (co-author Mark Teague)

Draw a large thought bubble on a piece of paper. In the bubble, have kids draw or write about a memorable dream they've had.

Piggies (co-author Don Wood)

Have kids create a new version of This Little Piggy Goes to Market. Have them assign each digit a new destination. Then trace their hands and write the new ditty around it.

Alphabet Adventure (co-author Bruce Wood)

Write each kid's name in large block letters and have them see what they can make each letter into for a fun art project.

The Little Mouse, The Red Ripe Strawberry,
and the Big Hungry Bear (co-author Don Wood)

Cut a strawberry out of red construction paper and a stem out of green. Use a cotton swab and paint to add seeds to the strawberry.

Also read:

By Audrey and Don Wood: Piggy Pie Po, The Tickloctopus, King Bidgood's in the Bathtub

By Audrey Wood: Balloonia, Blue Sky

Books by Jon Scieszka

★*The True Story of the Three Little Pigs*

Have kids choose their favorite fairy tale and re-tell it from a different character's point of view. Villains are always fun!

★*The Frog Prince, Continued*

Have kids choose a favorite fairy tale and write a story about what happened after the happily ever after.

Battle Bunny (co-author Mac Barnett)

Pick a popular story and have kids decide what they would change if they were in charge of telling it.

Robot Zot! (co-author David Shannon)

Make a robot with moveable limbs! Cut a square head, rectangle body, two arms, and two legs from cardboard and paint silver. Attach the head and limbs to the body using paper fasteners. Add eyes and a collection of bolts and other gadgets.

Cowboy and Octopus (co-author Lane Smith)

Have kids cut pictures from magazines to create their own characters and setting. They can cut and glue their collages and then write their story on the back.

Also read:

By Jon Scieszka and Lane Smith: The Stinky Cheese Man and Other Stupid Fairy Tales, Squids Will Be Squids, Maths Curse
By Jon Scieszka: The Book That Jack Wrote

Books by Judi Barrett

★*Cloudy with a Chance of Meatballs*

At the bottom of a piece of paper, write "Cloudy with a chance of

_____." Fill in the blank with things the kids would like to see it rain, then have them draw their unique weather phenomenon.

Cloudy with a Chance of Meatballs 2: Pickles to Pittsburgh

Get creative with food! Make giant meatballs, sunrise mashed potatoes, or foggy pea soup. Use the book as inspiration!

Cloudy with a Chance of Meatballs 3: Planet of Pies

Have kids draw their favorite scene from the book or their favorite dessert. Glue the drawing to construction paper and then cut it into pieces to create a personal puzzle.

The Marshmallow Incident

Use marshmallows to stamp paint, use them to create structures using toothpicks, or dip them in chocolate and sprinkles.

A Snake is Totally Tail

Practice using alliteration by having kids choose a quality they possess that starts with the same letter as their name. Once chosen, go around the room and try to guess the qualities.

Also read:

Animals Should Definitely Not Wear Clothing, Never Take a Shark to the Dentist, Things That Are Most in the World

Books by Patricia Polacco

Rechenka's Eggs

Based on traditional Ukrainian egg decorating, poke a small hole in each end of an egg and blow out the yolk and white. Bring them to class washed and dried. Have the kids color designs on the eggs in crayon and then dip in egg dye.

The Keeping Quilt

Give each kid a square of white cloth to decorate with fabric paint or markers. Sew all of the squares together and add a back (a sheet works great). Use the quilt in your class library.

The Lemonade Club

Make fresh squeezed lemonade. You will need lemons, a handheld juicer, a strainer, and some sugar as well as cups and a pitcher.

Thunder Cake

In a version of Red Light Green Light, use thunder, lightning, and rain instead. Have kids line up. If you say rain, they can walk, if you say thunder they can run, and if you say lightning they have to stop.

The Bee Tree

Have fun with honey! Bring in a real honeycomb, invite a beekeeper to class, and taste honey samples.

Also read:

Junkyard Wonders, When Lightning Comes in a Jar, Bun Bun Button, Meteor!, Ginger and Petunia

Quotes

"There is more treasure in books
than in all the pirate's loot on Treasure Island."
~Walt Disney

"The more that you read,
the more things you will know.
The more that you learn,
the more places you'll go."
~Dr. Seuss

"If you want your children to be intelligent,
read them fairy tales.
If you want them to be more intelligent,
read them more fairy tales."
~Albert Einstein

"If you are going to get anywhere in life
you have to read a lot of books."
~Roald Dahl

"No book is really worth reading at the age of ten
which is not equally (and often far more)
worth reading at the age of fifty."
~C.S. Lewis

"There are many little ways to enlarge your child's world.
Love of books is best of all."
~Jacqueline Kennedy

Activity

Create books from your kids' artwork. Each activity in this book that has a ★ next to it is perfect for adding to their book. The kids can then come up with their own titles and decorate the covers. Fold a full-size piece of construction paper in half and place the pages inside. Staple the spine or punch holes and let the kids secure with string.

Extras

Create a reading nook that everyone can enjoy. You will need a bookshelf or some other method of storing and displaying books. You can then add rugs, chairs, bean bags, blankets, etc. to make it a cozy place to read. Decorate the walls with favorite quotes, book-inspired artwork, or framed pages from old books.

Field Trip

Visit your local library! Set up a tour with the children's librarian so kids can get a behind-the-scenes look at what goes on at the library and how they can use it. They may even get a special story time! Before you go, send home library card applications for those that don't already have their own card.

Charity

Show kids how they can give back to their community by holding a book drive. Kids can bring in books they no longer read or purchase new books. Get others involved too! Accept donations of new or gently used children's books that can be given to shelters, hospitals, libraries, or sent overseas. Soldiers also like to receive books!

Holidays

January 23rd – National Reading Day
March 2nd – Read Across America Day
April 2nd – Hans Christian Andersen's birthday
April – National Library Week (3rd week)
May – Children's Book Week (3rd week)
September 6th – Read a Book Day
November – Picture Book Month

Jobs

An illustrator is just as important to the creation of a children's picture book as an author. Find out who drew the pictures in your kids' favorite books and learn more about them. Discuss the way an author and illustrator work together. Put the kids in pairs and have them create a storybook using this kind of teamwork.

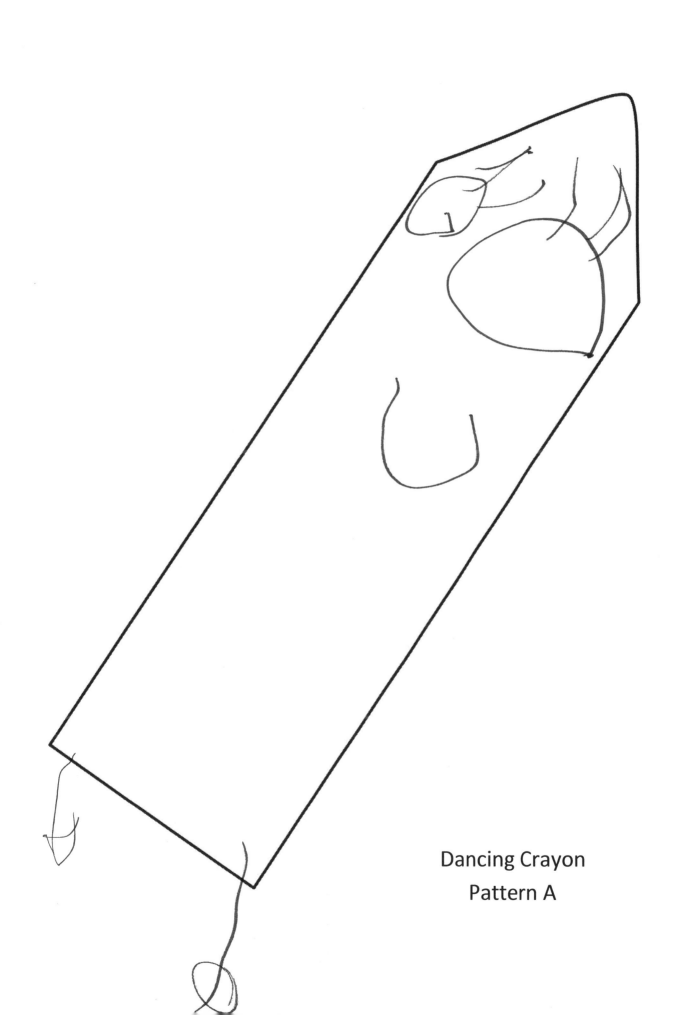

Dancing Crayon

Pattern A

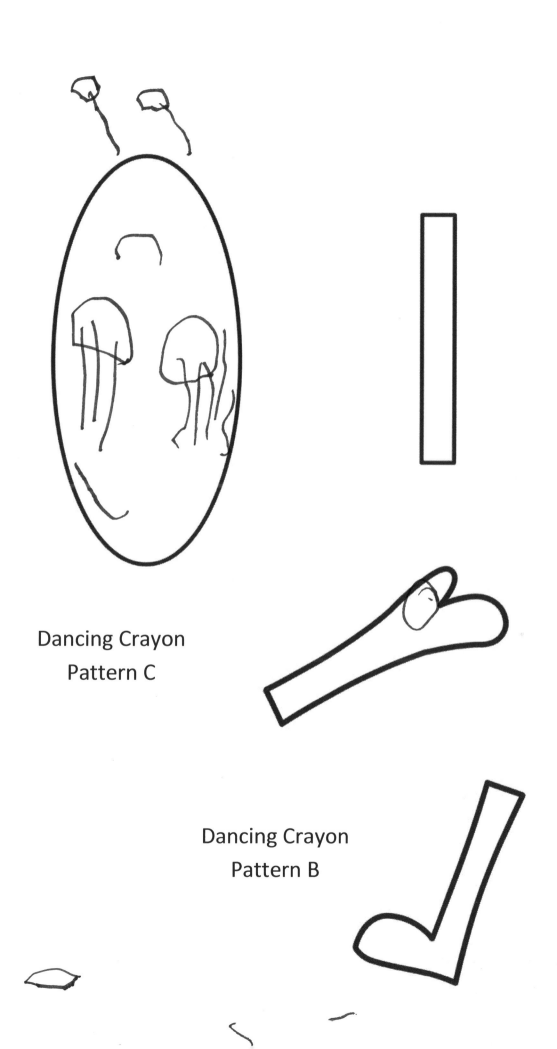

Dancing Crayon
Pattern C

Dancing Crayon
Pattern B

Crocodile Pattern
A and B

Toucan Pattern

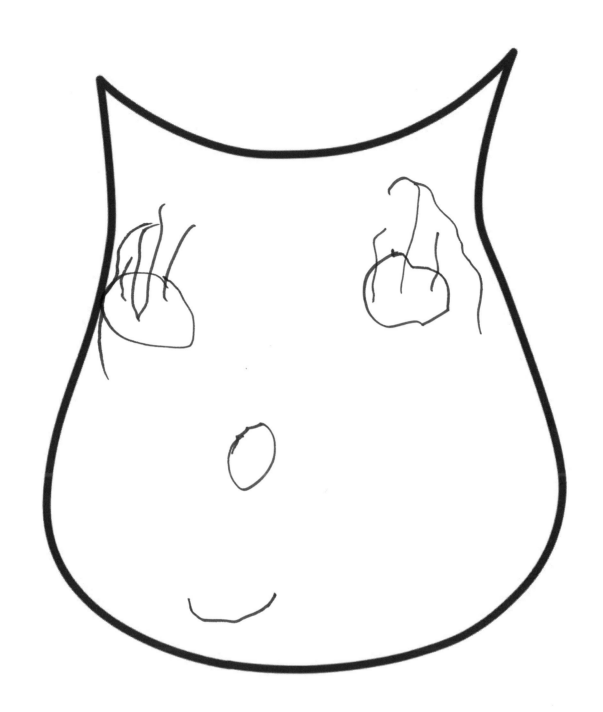

Owl Pattern A

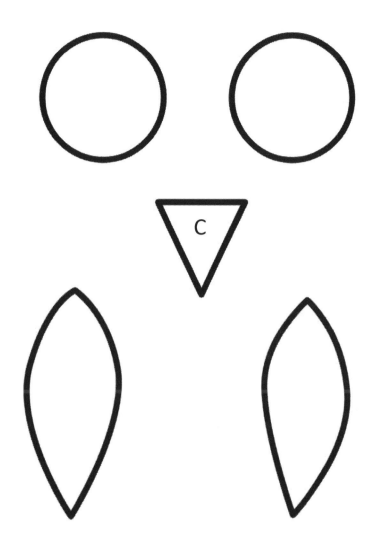

Owl Pattern B and C

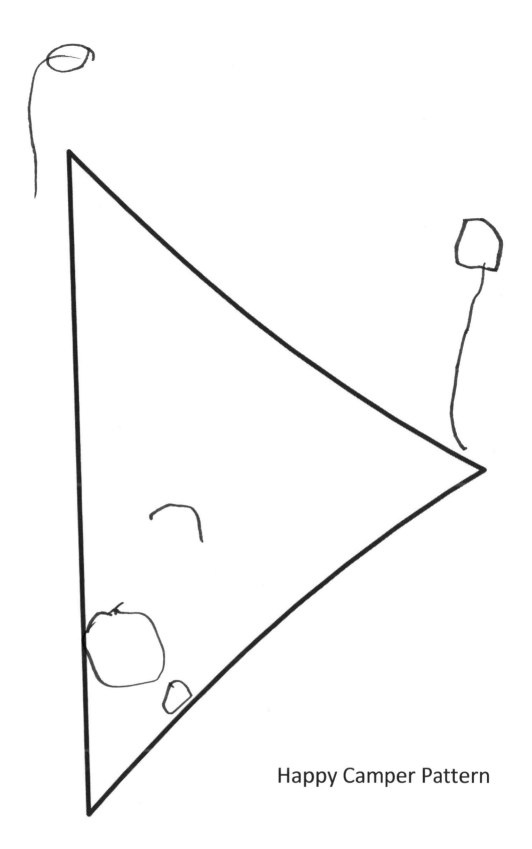

Happy Camper Pattern

Mermaid Pattern B

Mermaid Pattern A

Mermaid Pattern C

Starfish Pattern

Clothespin Fish Pattern

A and B

Sheep Pattern

Pig Pattern

Cupcake Pattern A

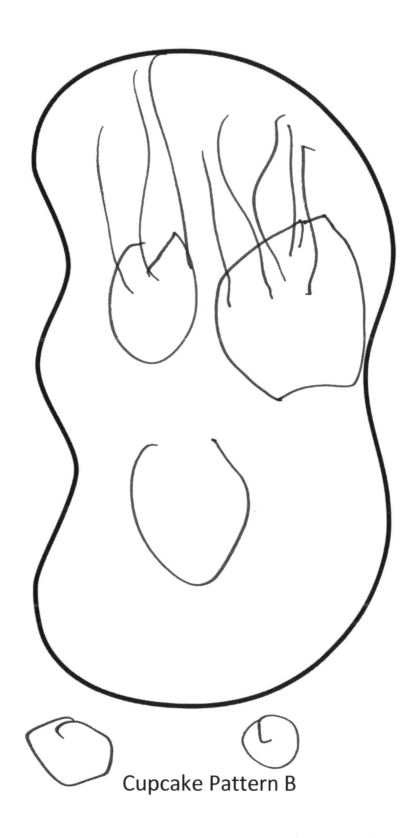

Cupcake Pattern B

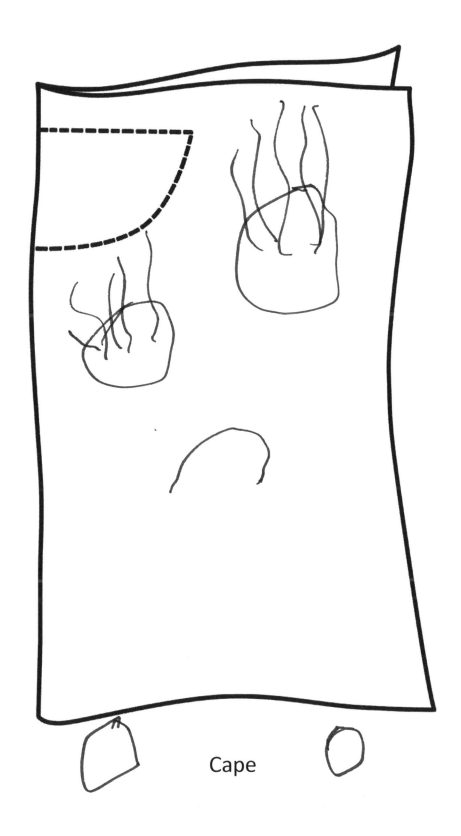

Cape

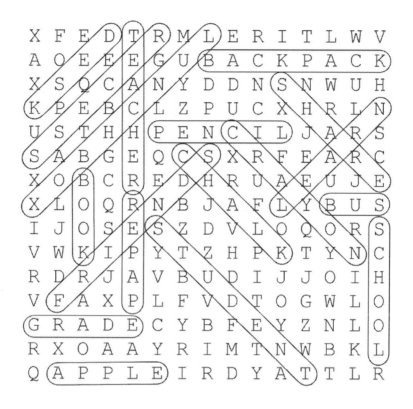

APPLE
BACKPACK
BOOK
BUS
CHALK
CRAYON
DESK
FRIENDS
GRADE

LEARN
LUNCHBOX
PAPER
PENCIL
RECESS
SCHOOL
SHARE
STUDENT
TEACHER

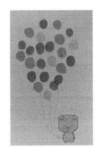

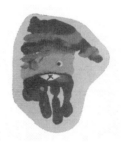

The Princess and the Pea

Resources

Cowboys and the Wild West
Gene Autry's Code of Honor
http://elvaquero.com/The_Cowboy_Code.htm

Camping and the Great Outdoors
The Great American Backyard Campout
www.backyardcampout.org

Jungle, Rainforest, Safari
Talking Crocodile Fun Facts
http://animal.discovery.com/reptiles/alligator-vs-crocodile.htm

Ahoy, Pirates!
Talk Like a Pirate Day
http://talklikeapirate.com
Petey Parrot Fun Fact
www.sciencekids.co.nz

Land of the Dinosaurs
Hungry T-Rex measurements
www.dimensionsinfo.com
Dino Fun Facts
www.sciencekids.co.nz

Under the Sea
Starfish Fun Facts
http://oceanservice.noaa.gov/facts/starfish.html

Space and Aliens
Space Weight
http://www.exploratorium.edu/ronh/weight/
Roswell, New Mexico
www.roswell-nm.gov
Space Holidays
www.holidays.net

Fun on the Farm
Muddy Pig Fun Fact
www.answers.com

Knights, Dragons, Princesses
The Princess and the Pea Fun Fact
www.hca.gilead.org.il
Pull Tab Charity / Ronald McDonald House
www.rmhc.org
Dragon Fruit
http://en.wikipedia.org/wiki/Pitaya

Eek, Monsters!
Pablo Picasso Quote
www.happybirthdayauthor.com
National Hot Fudge Sundae Day
www.holidayinsights.com

Books, Books, Books!
Quotes about reading
www.best-books-for-kids.com
Book Holidays
www.nationaldaycalendar.com

Notes

Allergies

Be aware and extremely careful of food allergies when working with kids. It is important to have allergy information before you try any of the recipes or food suggestions in this book.

Food Safety

When working with food, make sure that all surfaces have been sanitized and dishes and utensils are clean. Always wash your hands before touching food. Use extreme caution when utilizing knives and other sharp utensils. Do not let kids use any cooking utensils unsupervised. Knives should be for adult use only.

General Safety

Many of the activities in this book require the use of scissors and some require more unusual tools like hammers. No matter what tool you are using, be safe. Don't leave children unattended with scissors. Craft knives and hot glue guns should be for adult use only.

Suggestions

The books, films, field trips, etc. found in this collection are merely suggestions, and discretion should be used when choosing what is right for your particular group or child. Suggestions are not endorsements and are meant as ideas to spark creativity and enhance your experience.

Disclaimer

The author does not claim responsibility for any negative consequences resulting from using this book. The author also does not claim to be a certified teacher, a cowboy, a safari guide, an outdoor expert, a pirate, a paleontologist, an oceanographer, a superhero, an astronaut, a farmer, a princess (at least not officially), a fuzzy blue monster, or a personal friend of Dr. Seuss.

Acknowledgements

I want to thank all of the kids who have passed through my classroom over the last fourteen years for their constant inspiration. I also want to thank my brother, Erik, for designing parts of my layout and for putting up with my crazy projects. Thank you to my mom, Sharilyn, for being my second set of eyes when editing and introducing me to my love of working with kids. And thank you to my husband, Justin, for designing all of my clip art and encouraging me in my various endeavors.

About the Author

Rebecca Ross Klosinski is a writer and child care provider living on the central coast of California. She spends her mornings reporting local news and writing a travel column and her afternoons with a classroom full of kindergarteners. She enjoys exploring new places, finding ways for her kids to have fun, and hunting for adventures to share on her blog Rebecca's Big Adventure (www.rebeccasbigadventure.com).

To order a copy of Let's Have Fun!
visit www.amazon.com

You can also visit www.rebeccasrosswrites.com

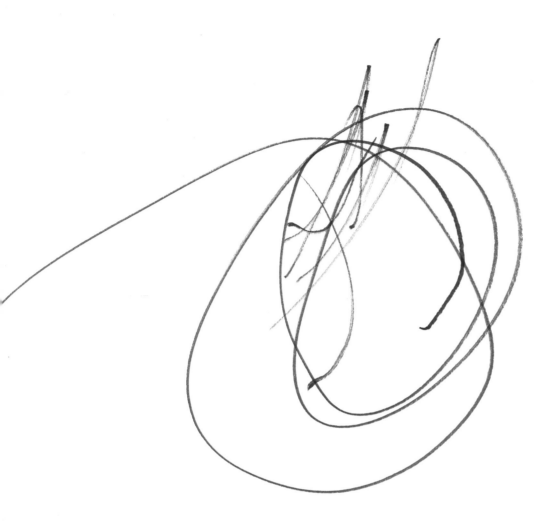

28230566R00130

Made in the USA
Lexington, KY
10 December 2013